Letters from Nowhere

Letters from Nowhere

by
Raymond Bernard

Translated by Joe Darwin Palmer, Ph.D.

Translation revised and edited by
Theodore J. Nottingham

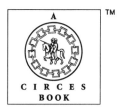

GLOBE PRESS BOOKS / NEW YORK

© Copyright 1992 CIRCES International, Inc.
All rights reserved.

Letters from Nowhere is translated from the French
Les Lettres de Nulle Part
by Raymond Bernard
Copyright 1990 Editions Rosicruciennes
56 rue Gambetta, 94195 Villeneuve-Saint-Georges - Cédex

Logo Design by Carolyn Meek

For reproduction rights, contact the publisher:
Globe Press Books, Inc.
P.O. Box 2045
Madison Square Station
New York, NY 10159-2045

This book is available at a special discount
when ordered in bulk quantities.

CIRCES Books are published
by Globe Press Books, Inc.
by arrangement with CIRCES International, Inc.

First Edition

ISBN 0-936385-32-4
Library of Congress Catalog Card No: 92-61534

10 9 8 7 6 5 4 3 2 1
Manufactured in the United States

Table of Contents

Preface to the French Edition vii

Introduction ix

1. *The Present Situation* 1

2. *Kamal Joumblatt, Grand Master of the Druzes* . . 17

3. *Rosicrucian Mystical Experience* 45

4. *The Spirit of India* 65

5. *India's Religious Landscape* 87

6. *Secret Ashrams* 113

7. *Grand Lamas of Tibet* 141

8. *The Bodhisattva and Tibetan Buddhism* 170

Preface to the French Edition

For a number of years, the internationally known esotericist Raymond Bernard sent letters to a large number of correspondents.

From the beginning, he called these texts *Letters from Nowhere*. He explained this title by the fact that they might be produced here and there during his frequent trips all around the world, and their subject matter was comprised of his experiences and encounters on these occasions. From anywhere on earth he would be able to present facts and arguments of universal meaning, which thereby took on a dimension which could be considered to come from everywhere or, indeed, from nowhere.

These letters had a great impact on those who were privileged to receive them. Their author, writing as if to a friend, expresses himself in easy, familiar language, as is the case in all private correspondence. In *Letters from Nowhere* he shares thoughts and travel notes, along with often surprising encounters with eminent, well-known people.

Raymond Bernard was frequently asked to gather and publish these letters which would certainly be of great value to many people, but his heavy responsibilities prevented him from doing so.

Recently, the author agreed to consider publication. He reread all of the *Letters from Nowhere* and carefully chose the ones to be included, eliminating those that had a bearing on personal matters. However, he kept everything that was of general interest to readers and the result was published in two volumes that will certainly meet the expectations of those who know Raymond Bernard, of those who have only heard about him, and of those who do not yet know him.

We present this book with great happiness. We hope the *Letters from Nowhere* give you as much comfort and understanding as they have given to those who had access to them in the past. This is our friendly wish for you as you begin reading what will without doubt be a source of fruitful personal reflection.

The Editor

Introduction

When I accepted the task of writing an Introduction to Raymond Bernard's *Letters from Nowhere* I asked myself "Now what can I say to the American public that would at once present the essence of the man and, at the same time, do justice to his thoughts"? I pondered for a very long time and then one morning I awoke with the answer! "Simply write of the man you know and the reasons for his many travels and his extraordinary experiences on the way!" So that is exactly what I will do. But I will also allow the man himself to speak in his own behalf. Therefore, from time to time, I will choose from his voluminous writings some of his own words.

I first met Raymond Bernard in 1972 on one of his many voyages to Canada—specifically French Canada. At the time I was a "young" student in the esoteric movement currently known as The Rosicrucian Order AMORC and had been skeptical of the many flowery phrases and epithets used by my "elder" Brothers and Sisters in describing the man. Surely, no one man could possibly possess all those qualities—and in such abundance!

He was in Canada on official business as the Grand Master of L'Ordre de la Rose+Croix, responsible for the French-speaking members of AMORC throughout the world. And although the Lodge to which I belonged was English-speaking he nevertheless came to visit with us and to share with us some of his vast knowledge in the realm of Esoteric Studies. It was a devilishly hot evening and the air-conditioning was unable to keep pace with the temperature outside plus the "heat" that was being generated inside by the enthusiasm of the sizeable crowd that had come to see him. As a consequence, at a formal gathering during the course of the evening a young mother-to-be succumbed to the heat and, as is so often the case with human nature, the vast majority of those present simply stared at the limp body of our prostrated Sister with a mixture of curiosity, amazement, and wonder. Finally someone moved. Someone had decided to assist our Sister to leave the room and to get some fresh air. Still the majority stared. Suddenly there was a voice—clear, calm, gentle, firm and French: "Instead of staring at our Sister in wonderment, send her your prayers and good thoughts!" It was the voice of Raymond Bernard.

Suddenly I was forced to consider the possibility that perhaps my "elder" brothers and sisters might just have been right about this man after all. This was to be the first of many experiences I was destined to have with the direct gentleness of Raymond Bernard.

Later that evening, in a less formal setting, I was to learn of an incident which others might characterize as coincidental, but which for me, because of the frequency with which such "coincidences" occur in his life, speaks of the openness of the man—an openness which in some mysterious way, serves as a sort of attractive force. Over and over we find evidence of these "coincidences" in his various writings which largely chronicle his inward and outward voyages. But more on that later.

Returning to the incident of the "coincidence", it was the custom at the time to present a visiting dignitary with a token of appreciation as a momenta of the occasion. The leader of our group, being conscious of this fact and, at the same time wishing to express his gratitude for a bit of good fortune which had recently come into his life, decided to do something extraordinary. On an intuition he decided to search among the many antique stores of Old Montreal for something old and appropriate. Almost as if drawn by some invisible magnet he entered an old store and was immediately attracted to a particular painting. He picked up the painting and, struck by the signature of the artist, he stood transfixed for a moment or two in total astonishment. The artist's signature on the painting was that of none other than Dr. H. Spencer Lewis who, in 1915, founded the Rosicrucian Order AMORC!

If he were surprised at hearing the unusual circumstances surrounding the finding of this painting, Raymond Bernard did not show it. Instead he graciously thanked us all, accepted his gift, and placed it on display so that all present might see it. Obeying the inner law: "As you receive, so also must you give!", he then proceeded to speak to us of the advantages of developing our inner faculties so that we may live more fulfilling lives with less frustration and trauma and, in so doing, enabling ourselves to become more effective in rendering service to others. My "elders" were looking better and better by the minute!

How does such a personality develop? Is it merely a matter of genes or a matter of environment and chance occurrences? I had often wondered about the circumstances of birth and family that would contribute to the development of a Raymond Bernard. He himself admits to having been born into very fortunate circumstances both materially and spiritually. Thus, it appears that his remarkable openness, a decidedly "feminine" trait esoterically speaking, is attributable to the openness of the very strong females who have populated his life since birth. Of these he speaks often of his mother and her openness to the liberal ideas of her time; an English Professor by the name of Mrs. Edith Lynn who taught him English and was his first teacher in esoterism; Jeanne Guesdon from whom he inherited the mantle of responsibility as head of the French Rose+Croix in 1956; and, of course, his charming wife, Yvonne, who continues to have a positive influence in his life. In profane terms such remarkable openness to any and all eventualities might be characterized as fearlessness. But in my view it is more a matter of self-confidence born of having faced fear in its many disguises and having deprived it of its power to influence his inner attitudes, or direct his outer actions. Interestingly, it is precisely because of his openness and self-confidence that others are drawn to him and present to his consciousness the experiences he shares with us all, through his inner and outer "travels."

Having said all of this it is now time to let the man speak for himself. Through his inner "voyages" he has been an instrument for the transmission of many messages from the "Masters" whom he has carefully defined as personifications of levels of inner awareness to which we may each aspire. Thus, speaking with the voice of one of these "Masters" in *Messages from the Celestial Sanctum,* he expresses the profound convictions of his soul. Regarding the practice of visualization he has the following to say:

> "To visualize means 'to see inwardly' and it is evident that one cannot arrive at this 'inward seeing' without first having developed the faculty of objective observation. There are many who look without seeing... The mistake that the disciple generally makes and which, tragically, impedes inner development, is dissipation of effort even though the search is conducted with the very best of intentions... Anyone who dissipates his efforts in such activities as thoughtless reading, or the study of various techniques is certain to get little or no results except the illusion of an overburdened mind and the disappointment of repeated setbacks... Knowledge may be obtained from many authentic sources provided that these sources do not teach different techniques... Consequently the first step toward effectiveness in the initiatic life...is the careful choice of a technique... How many are there who err in psychic matters! They are not able to free themselves from

the matrix of their dreams. The emotions they seek are impregnated with vague sentimentality. In fact, they seek pleasure in sentimentality. What they call 'knowledge' consists of fantasies of the intellect or of an emotional satisfaction in which all sorts of obscure sentiments are mixed in with ignorance... Visualization assumes that a choice has been made and a technique definitely adopted... Knowledge of principles is useless if it remains purely theoretical."

Insofar as the technique of "Entering the Silence" is concerned, he alerts us to the rigors of mental discipline which are required if one ever hopes to avail him or herself of the benefits of such a practice. Thus:

"The practice of *The Silence* is a frequent obligation of the mystic. Overcoming mental restlessness, putting aside every exterior thing, one enters into oneself for a few moments to glean direction and Light from the center where the essence of all spiritual, mental, and material ideas converge in harmonious combination... To enter *The Silence* then is to participate no longer; no longer to have objective consciousness of the mental or physical processes which continue uninterrupted throughout the whole of human life."

Raymond Bernard holds that thought is the master of the body and, as a consequence, healing and thought are inextricably linked. In *Messages from the Celestial Sanctum* he declares:

"Creation is a breath, a continuous contraction and relaxation which man marks in cycles, but which he still does not fully understand. Thus life is one...all is Life! ...Thought is the master of the body, thus we understand why healing requires confidence which is itself a powerful form of positive thought... Evil does not exist of itself."

As for those who are concerned that the negative aspects of the personality are in and of themselves an impediment to spiritual advancement, he has the following to say:

> "The fundamental quality of the mystic is to be himself. He does not seek hypocritically to conceal his negative aspects in order to display to the eyes of the world only the positive. He knows that the greatest Masters themselves possess this double polarity as long as they are incarnated, and that in being themselves they give to others the greatest lesson and the finest example."

As to his writing style, in *Strange Encounters* he cautions us that:

> "To understand certain subjects it is not enough to read them. One must experience them! And that is why I have adopted this form of writing. The result is that this manuscript is partially allegorical and partially also relates to facts... It is not, however, my intention to reveal here that which is in the realm of personal mystical experience..."

Therefore, in reading *Letters from Nowhere* it would be well to remember that there are certain irrefutable facts around which certain ideas are woven. It is well to remember also that these *Letters* were written with the specific purpose of transmitting to the reader certain esoteric information. And although they were written at a time when he was still responsible for the welfare of the organization which he represented, this fact, nevertheless, did not prevent him from expressing the universality of his views. In this regard what he had to say in 1969 in *The Secret Houses of the Rose-Croix* concerning the fate of all traditional organizations in the New Era is revealing.

> "The esoteric structure of ancient forms are breaking up everywhere and in the new cycle their role in the reformed

structure will be different and, in comparison with what it was in the past, it will be incontestably diminished. It is up to the traditional organizations to make the change, and this fact explains why the High Council is so interested in them without intervening in their activities, their traditions, or their way of operating. Indeed our vigilance leads us to protect these organizations from the dangers caused by the perverted actions of some people who need to satisfy the exigencies of their ego, fascinated as they are by the false grandeur of apparent advantage. In truth and in fact, although each traditional organization is different one from the other, on the Traditional Path all are equal with respect to that which they must attain."

Since these words were written over twenty years ago we have all occasion to witness the disintegration of many traditional structures both in matters of mundane affairs as well as in the esoteric arena. Knowing in the depths of his being that insofar as his sphere of activity was concerned there was nothing he could do to change the course of events, Raymond Bernard opted instead to create a vehicle of expression in accord with the changing times—times in which an appreciable number of students are moved to express in constructive action in the outer world all that they have been accumulating and contemplating inwardly for years. CIRCES International is the vehicle which has been created to fill this special need.

Through his numerous "outer" travels Raymond Bernard has touched the lives of many—the great and the not-so-great. Because of this he has innumerable friends—friends in high places and low. In addition to *Letters from Nowhere* the accounts of his many "outer" journeys are chronicled in such works as *Strange Encounters, Secret Meetings in Rome, The Secret Houses of the Rose-Croix,* and others. Thus it is in *Secret Meetings in Rome* that we find an account of some of the facts surrounding his mandate to revive "The Order of the Temple" (Templar Tradition) adapted to the needs of our time. As early as 1969 he had already initiated experiments designed to indicate and perfect the mode of expression of "Templar Chivalry" for the New Era. And having retired from his official obligations in 1986, two years later he received directives to create CIRCES International with its inner core of Templarism and The School of Pythagoras.

If I had but one gift to offer each Student on The Path it would be the gift of knowing Raymond Bernard as I do. But given the fact that for the overwhelming majority of you this is not likely to occur, I can only hope that in reading his *Letters from Nowhere* each of you will at least capture a little of the essence of the man. And if, in the future, you should have the opportunity to read our official translations of his other writings, then I would strongly recommend that you do so. It could conceivably change your life!

                       Onslow H. Wilson, Ph.D.
                       Chancellor - CIRCES International, Inc.
                       Post Office Box 279
                       Plainfield, Indiana 46168
                       Sunday, July 19, 1992

ND# 1
JANUARY 1977

The Present Situation

Dear Friends,

The *Letters from Nowhere* give me the opportunity, every four months, to speak to numerous friends about the most diverse questions. I will deal with both traditional subjects and other issues. But I do not intend to limit myself to these areas. You will accompany me on journeys that I have undertaken and even if for some reason I cannot go into details, I will not leave out any interesting encounters. In short, I will tackle questions that aren't usually included in traditional studies, such as family, social, and even economic problems. If necessary, I will give practical advice. It must be understood that for all the subjects I bring up, the opinions expressed are my personal ones. You may share my opinions or not. The choice is yours. In any event, be sure that I will always be aware of different perspectives, even opinions opposite to my own. I know and respect these opposite opinions. It is not my intention to enter into polemical arguments. When I give advice, or express a point of view, my purpose is never to convince anyone, and I may even express ideas utterly opposed to my deepest convictions, only to make people think. This is why, in my *Letters from Nowhere,* I use and will continue to use the personal pronoun "I" even though it demonstrates the limitations of the mind in the play of its arguments anchored in a present which flees as soon as it has appeared. I may at times contradict myself, affirming something one day, and claiming its opposite the next, thereby revealing the impermanence of the moment and the truth of the permanence of universal Thought and the Oneness of Life. This is a traditional technique, and for many people its effects will be felt rapidly. To awaken and elevate the powerful mechanisms of the Self is one of the most necessary and worthwhile effects of traditional intellectual and moral education. To a certain degree the *Letters from Nowhere* will also have this effect.

To conclude these first remarks let me say that these messages will be written in a style as simple and clear as possible. In other words, I am not looking for literary effect. By definition letters like these require familiar phrases. They establish a privileged rapport, even an intimacy, between the writer and the reader. I will be to each of you only a brother writing to members of his family, a spiritual family whose bonds are stronger and narrower than those of blood.

In this first letter I would like to share with you some thoughts about the state of the world we live in now. I'm sure that I'll have to come back to this subject often in order to deepen our understanding of the many elements that make it up. But for today it will be sufficient just to take a quick look at the conditions that humanity has plunged into, the smallest eddy of which affects us all, for good or for evil. I know that I'm fundamentally an incorrigible optimist. I can't even meditate on death, as I do every day, without my thoughts returning insistently to life. Black storm clouds always make me turn to the ever-present sun that soon will be shining again. If obstacles present themselves, I can already see a future in which they have been overcome, and I believe that problems have value only in their solutions. The brevity of individual life and the brevity of the moment, in which every instant disappears after giving birth to the following one, relativize all that was given the illusion of permanence by our thoughts. And I truly believe that if everyone looked on things in this way problems would be looked at from the outside, evaluated for what they really are, better faced, and quickly resolved. This way no one would be affected by anything but transitory emotions. In other words, every day should be lived to the fullest, and at the same time put in the perspective of tomorrow, and even of the far future, because everyone's inevitable death includes all solutions by putting an end to all problems. Seen in this way, existence and its context of peace or torment take their rightful place without indifference ever prevailing. However, such an attitude that individually justifies itself by the effectiveness it gives to personal existence, by the well-being it causes, and by the interior peace of which it is the essential key, would be unrealistic in relation to the whole world and to humanity. This is what we must see, examine, observe and experience. We can, in spite of everything, remain optimistic and have confidence and hope.

But it would be an irresponsible attitude to ignore the conditions of the human situation, as though their consequences could only be accepted and submitted to like a decoration that generations have contributed and that we each perpetuate in an artificial existence whose influence is only too real. The reversed image that the eye perceives seems right side up without our being conscious of our having corrected it. On the other hand, if the world, in spite of our doubts, seems perfect in its incessant chain of causes and effects, isn't it really quite the opposite, with no child innocent enough to awaken humankind by shouting that "the Emperor has no clothes on"? Let us live, with the mass of humanity, with the truth of our perceptions, without questioning ourselves over the substance of our imperfections. Basing our analysis on purely human science, let us observe without judging, delaying our conclusions until a later letter.

According to certain ancient traditions, humankind is in the last phase of a four-phase cycle that has lasted several thousand years. We are at the end of the Age of Obscurity. These traditions affirm that at the end of this age a *manvantara*, that is, the turning of the whole cycle of four phases is complete. At this point, the Great Judgement will take place, in which the souls reincarnated since the beginning of the cycle are definitively judged and sentenced either to annihilation or to participation in the beginning of the next cycle. The Age of Obscurity, or the Age of Decline, or yet, according to Hindu wisdom, the Age of Conflict began about five thousand years ago during a war brought on by the Aryan invasion of the Indian sub-continent. This war between the natives and the invaders is known in history as the War of Mahabarata. One could conclude, in the light of these traditions, that the end of humanity as it now exists is near. The *Chronicle of the Future*, a work that dates from the dawn of time, that is, of our time, reveals that the dark age we are living in is leading to a complete collapse of everything, and this age will end in a catastrophe that will destroy humanity. This same work explains that this catastrophe will consist of an under-sea explosion, a kind of volcano that in Sanskrit is called *Mule's Head*. This volcano will burst out of the sea-bed and destroy all the life on earth. According to the *Chronicle of the Future*, very few survivors will enter the new cycle with the Golden Age or the Age of Truth, a phase of great wisdom, followed by the Threefold Age, and finally the Age Beyond the Two, which will precede a new dark age similar to the one whose agony we know so well. Humanity has already appeared on earth six times, developing itself and achieving considerable scientific and technical prowess. But the final catastrophe is upon us. We will be followed by seven more appearances of humankind on earth, then all will be finished and the earth will be a desert. Keeping this *Chronicle* in mind, let us look at the conditions that prevail—for only a while, according to these traditions—in this dark age of ours. To do this, let us look at the observances of a modern writer, Alain Danielou:

"The further we advance in this age of conflict, the more man's virtue is degraded. He is becoming irresponsible, corrupt, egotistical. The sciences that used to be reserved for those who knew how to use them with wisdom have been given over to common men who do not have the discernment necessary to use them without dreadful results. Everyone is trying to replace people better-qualified than themselves instead of making the effort to get to know their own nature and their proper place in society. In the resulting social disorder what is valued is ambition, not capability. The good soldier becomes the hated tyrant, the good worker becomes an incapable minister, the prince becomes a rotten businessman, the literate person becomes a servile employee.

"The interior spiritual life is devoid of knowledge, and religion thus becomes blind faith and an instrument of persecution. All the religions begun in the age of conflict are part of social revolutions, and their aberrant dogmas are used as instruments by temporal powers to establish their domination. Only the mystics, in their isolation from the world, know how to use their intuition to make contact with the eternal realities, but they are most often ignored or persecuted."

It is evident that such a state of affairs develops progressively during the five thousand years that constitute an age. And, if we believe the old traditions, the final process has now begun. Naturally, the history of past centuries shows clearly that the beginning of the descent to our own times seems to support the millenarian theory of cycles. But we should also take into account the present facts in the light of the universal law of karma. It should be possible, in this case, to link karma to the notion of *manvantara* and *Great Judgement,* or further to place our own times in a phase of pure transition toward a new and more advanced world. The second is more optimistic, and is therefore the one I am more inclined to follow. However, I will choose the first because it seems to me infinitely more logical, even if I have reservations and doubts on the subject of the Great Judgement.

Let us make an effort to picture the conditions of our times from this point of view. In a relatively few years an upset of unimaginable amplitude has taken place. Inviolable values of twenty-five years ago have given way or are dying, and radical changes have taken place in family and social life. Churches that were all powerful for centuries have proceeded, under the pressure of new circumstances, to undergo shattering conversions into that which they formerly opposed, throwing the faithful into confusion and desolation. What used to be a sin is a sin no longer, and intolerant persecution is giving way to weakness and laxity. Politically, the efforts to adjust to a different world are slower than the changes taking place, and most curious is certainly the artificial life that intelligent men, whose worth is unquestionable, try to give to outmoded ideologies of a bygone century, in particular to Marxism.

Most people ignore the fact that this term marks old and ineffective theories that might have been revolutionary at one time but now in today's world have the look and smell of death. It would be better to find a new term for an ideology really in harmony with the vague hopes of our times rather than imposing on people the attempts to revive a cadaver. As for liberalism, even advanced liberalism, there is a great risk that it will finally turn out to be a mirage, even if it is generous and seems to be making progress in certain regards. I sincerely believe that, given on one hand the inconsequential ideologies that are really useless to a humanity profoundly torn from self-knowledge, and on the other hand all the illusory programs, we have to appeal to people themselves as long as people are true and sincere, and insofar as they can provide their good will. For it is this good will which is the only instrument available to distinguish the real needs of our times in the final drama of this dark age.

Anyone who looks hard at what is happening cannot fail to be impressed by the contradictions of these times. Travel is quicker than ever before. We get the news as soon as it is broadcast. Telecommunications make images and voices immediately available. These are only a few examples that we could multiply to infinity. But, at the same time, what do we see? A disunited world, countries shut up behind rigid boundaries, violent nationalism everywhere, a bitter economic struggle, a build-up of deadly arms that could reduce the planet to cinders, a withdrawal into regionalism, a preoccupation with class and corporate interests, a safeguarding of acquired advantages, and many other contradictions of these times. All this reveals what can be called planetary egotism, with all that it implies: indifference, callousness, and an appetite for pleasure now at all costs. Undoubtedly, the tragic reason for these present conditions, unless it is the consequence, is naturally the mass confusion about the mystery of the afterlife. God really is dead for a great number of people, and He can only be resurrected for those whose anguish drives them to Him. Such a breakdown is the result of a faith that has been weak for centuries and of one imposed on people from the outside, by the State, or by dogma and extreme ritualism that became, not in itself but in its effects, superstition and obscurantism. The Kingdom of God was not sought within the self, that is, at the level of the purest spirituality, but outside the self on the mental level and through the objective world. At the same time, in many cases, in order to impose and maintain itself, religion had to depend on established authority to such an extent that it participated in its excesses and was quickly caught in its own snares, becoming a docile object in the hands of power rather than influencing decisions for the better.

I am often asked whether atheism isn't simply a reaction to this state of affairs. For most people religion and God coincide in all respects, so to refuse religion implies refusing God at the same time. Moreover, since religion became the expression and guardian of the ruling class, of power and money, it was inevitable that it would give off antagonism. The more rigid and monolithic it became, the more the forces against it were strengthened. Without getting into politics, isn't it proof of my assertions that wherever Catholicism was powerful, Communism was too, and the inverse—Communism never really took over in those countries where the Church was not powerful. This is something for the historians and the sociologists to think about. This historical matter is not very important in regard to the absolute, even if it did play a part in shaping today's world. After all, we have seen that Marxism is a term emptied of its original meaning. Today it represents only a form of argument.

The purpose of these observations is to point up the contradictions inherent in these times and the uselessness of solutions based on outmoded ideologies. If we accept the ideas in the old *Chronicle of the Future*, it can be said that all the pieces are in place. Humanity has not kept in step with the times. We have, instead, been almost exclusively preoccupied with our material development. What could have been a transitional stage on the way to a new age is looking more and more like a tragic, universal drama. It is clear that each cyclical age is a time of action and evolution and if people were more clearer sighted, they could have made use of our era as a difficult journey to a new dawn. Our knowledge of the dangers should have enabled us to surmount most of the obstacles in the way. But we did not do that. We put up with the cycle and progressively, through elimination, we are coming face to face with our judgement.

The forces of hatred have crystallized, and the world awaits. Clashing ideologies have set the stage for karmic action. Let's look briefly at the state of the world, not from a political point of view, but according to the facts. There are three great currents affecting the peoples of the whole earth. Other forces are effects of these currents. Two of these currents appear to be the same ideology on the surface, but express themselves in two radically opposite aspects: Soviet and Chinese Communism. The third current is, of course, Capitalism, as badly named as the first two. Actually I use these terms just to express the global situation. I could have referred to Russia, China, the United States, the three countries which are the poles of the circumstances of our time.

It is unrealistic for other people to feel independent of these three poles. The hope of national independence is in fact just a pipe-dream. You don't have to be a statesman to realize this. Even the new European Community will not be independent and free. We would like to think that eventually united Europe will be a reality, but it too will be anchored in one of these three poles.

Here then is the end of our dark age, of the age of conflicts, in all its tragic simplicity: three powerful groups whose only purpose is to control the world. Evidently, if there should be a final conflict, as the *Chronicle of the Future* insists, putting an end to present-day humanity, the adjustment will come about also from the three pieces put in place by the play of the individual, national, and world-wide karma. Additionally, past experience allows us to understand that the detonator will not be some direct and immediate action on the part of one of these three currents. It will probably happen because of some obscure but powerful rivalry, most likely in the Middle East, where a more-or-less-secret, veiled struggle is going on among diverse groups. The blow up should start between the East and the West, with China intervening only when the two adversaries are exhausted by a battle that neither side can win. Logically, in order for the new age to be established the third and final current cannot win. At that point a new start will be made to regroup what remains of humanity. The new leaders, basing their actions on authentic, new values, will finally find victory in throwing off what remains of the past age that ended in horror.

That is but a brief sketch of what a mystical analysis of the conditions of our times allows us to understand concerning the karma that present-day humanity must face. I could be much more precise, but it would take many more pages for me to go more deeply into certain aspects of this drama. I will have occasion to return to this topic in later letters. My purpose today is to direct your attention to a particular situation from which a cycle has to play itself out. As such, what I have written has nothing to do with prophecy. It is about verifications and logical observations. Naturally, on this basis any conclusion is possible. What is important to know in such matters is not the how but the why, and this why can be seen in advance by looking at the explanations given here. Any further expansion would be unrealistic speculation and so would go beyond my intention. I have had to refer to ideologies because the subject forces me to, but I have not, for all that, committed a political act. However, it was inevitable for me to express opinions about these ideologies, and I have done it from a wide point of view, without taking sides. I regret it very much that the people responsible for the perpetuation of these ideologies had not been inspired to work out a platform of entirely new ideas that would meet the needs of present-day humanity at this point in our evolution.

But things are what they are, or more precisely, what they must be in the universal cycle of creation. It is worth noting, to simplify further, that the bases of present ideologies were crystallized sharper than ever before on the two motives that gave life to the whole dark age: self interest, whether of an individual, group, or a political party, and money, both aiming at another point or element: power, something humankind has always been starved for. These two motives will be the topic of another letter.

Is the situation as I have described it here without hope, or is it just a simple step of transition toward the new age? I will conclude this message on that point.

Karma, the law of compensation, is, by definition, a lesson to learn. Karma can be positive or negative, according to the thought or act that gives it being. As we understand karma, even happiness must be experienced correctly in order for it not to turn into its opposite. Furthermore, there are many sides to karma. In particular, it can affect the individual, the family, the nation, and the whole world. So the karma of an individual is closely allied to that of his family, his nation, and that of the world in which he lives. As in everything, we must go back to the supreme principle of Unity, and remember that all is in All. Abstraction remains the primary key to the ensemble of the manifestations of the created. Consequently, if we raise ourselves out of the worldly state of karma up to the source of thought, which is outside of time, we then have the possibility of affecting the working out of the karma of the end of this cycle. It is evident that for this to happen, it is only on the spiritual level that humanity will understand the circumstances we are in and the lessons that these circumstances imply. There is no other way for the proofs of the accumulated karma to be brought to a bearable stage. Remember that it is not solely a question of *knowing* what is karmically foreseen, but of *feeling* it intensely. And there is the problem. Such a collective awareness is difficult to bring about.

But we must also remember that humankind is not an isolated element in the infinity of that which is visible and invisible. Whatever we undertake for our own well-being and that of others must be done with faith. Above all, even if we alone are responsible for the adverse conditions that we encounter, we must never doubt that our Creator is goodness and mercy, with the result that if we help ourselves we will also be helped by Heaven. When all is said and done, it is not worth the trouble to be preoccupied with how the world's karma will be revealed, when this revelation will take place, or why. You don't philosophize with the sick; you treat them. The initiation into these mysteries would be only vanity with a falsified purpose if it served merely to glorify some individuals. Its unique value is found in service carried out *in secret and with humility*. The truly initiated one leaves the skeptics to their doubts, the intellectuals to their sophistries, the opposition to their incessant mental agitations. He has been through all this before, by necessity, in the process of becoming a mystic. In reaching this sublime degree of silence he realizes that the time has come for action and service. He remembers the simple assumption: *all that is below is like all that is above.* In this enlightened state, he lives this within himself, knowing that what he sees around him is an exact replica of the invisible. To try to help humanity, imperilled with hazards, he must direct his attention to the world's aura.

This aura consists of vibrations, just as conscious thought consists of vibrations of a definite quality that connect with and act on other vibrations. The world's aura is filled with thoughts and actions that took place over hundreds and thousands of years. Even if this aura is balanced in its double polarity, positive and negative, it is the positive side of this polarity that keeps the world on an even keel. A few powerful, positive thoughts and acts keep the equilibrium. Without these vibrations, all would be chaos. This small number of positive vibrations is created, first of all, by the initiated and the mystics and, secondly, by those who pray and pay homage to the Divinity in some way or other.

Finally, all good thoughts, just actions, and attitudes of compassion, love, and solidarity contribute to the positive side of the world's aura. But if you feel that the balance of this double polarity is barely maintained, you are feeling the strength of the negative vibrations that humanity is generating. The vital equilibrium is easily broken! It is enough to turn us into fatalists, as if circumstances and facts are inevitable, and all we can do is to wait in resignation. That would indeed accelerate their arrival, for fear and the certainty that bad things are going to happen simply generate additional negative vibrations of a terrifying power.

That is why I prefer the peaceful assurance of the skeptic, for it has no effect on existing conditions, and makes them no worse than they already are. To a certain extent such assurance may even have a positive influence on these conditions. Moreover, in my opinion, it is better to admit what the old wisdom has transmitted to us, and to contemplate events in the way foreseen by the great sages of the dawn of time in the *Chronicle of the Future,* always with the important reservation that the final catastrophe of an age is avoidable, and a new cycle can succeed an old one by a simple transition, even if it is somewhat unsettled. I am more and more convinced that I share the certainty of those for whom a trial is never imposed without being accompanied by the strength to overcome it. But it is clear that if such hope is allowed in the circumstances of this final age, it must be achieved through human effort. The boiling up of ideas that we are witnessing, the confused yearning for spirituality, which is finding expression in a thousand ways and causing the formation of groups and movements that have no value or effectiveness, much less goodwill, the springing into life of initiatic orders and the fanatic, underhanded opposition to them demonstrate that humanity is not abandoned to itself and that every possible assistance is given to us. It is humanity that has the choice to remain master of its future. It is up to a minority that has been made ready and prepared itself, on whom the responsibility falls to make the necessary efforts. This minority is made up of initiates, of mystics, of those who are moving forward in knowledge and self-improvement. Their duty lies in service to humankind from the beginning of their development even if it appears that each individual's progress seems to be relegated to second place.

The present situation and the one we see coming in the future must not be feared. Nor must we adopt a wait-and-see policy. The situations must be faced, whatever the eventualities, arousing in us the will to act, to give spiritual help. It is certain that a constructive and effective work has always been accomplished in this sense by numerous traditional organizations as well as by individual seekers. Certain traditional rituals provide for periods of meditation, in the course of which positive thoughts are radiated by each of the participants toward the whole surface of the earth. Other rituals direct positive vibrations toward world leaders. During personal research the seeker does the same thing, whether he is aware of it or not. The simple fact of being sincerely engaged on a path toward the light, of whatever sort, reinforces the positive aspects of the human environment. However, during critical periods, these are not sufficient. At those times concerted actions are imperative. This is why those who are aware that our world is in a critical period, and that the vibratory power of thinking makes a difference, must cooperate, as has been mentioned above. This altruistic service rendered for a great cause takes a lot of effort and perseverance, but it is simple and doesn't take time. It consists merely of entering into silence one or two times a day, of a brief meditation that can last several minutes or only two or three seconds during which you direct positive thoughts to the world's aura, radiating them outside yourself all around the earth. Visualization is useful in accomplishing this. The earth can be imagined as a sphere in space surrounded by a gloomy halo. Then a deep breath is taken, with the idea that in breathing in, a positive energy is attracted into oneself. And the moment one exhales, this energy rises toward the world's aura, which it helps to purify. At that moment one must see the aura of the earth as clearer and more brilliant. This period of work ends by diffusing thoughts of love, peace and consolation over all the earth. Moreover, anytime a tragic event occurs anywhere in the world, as soon as possible there must be immediate action, not of adopting an afflicted and powerless attitude, but of sending positive vibrations to that place, and of proceeding then, as soon as possible, to such a meditation.

    This must become a daily effort. Finally, we must make every effort for each of us to become a real instrument of peace. For this to happen the fundamental rule to observe is *not to judge*. To want to participate in a work of love in the service of others, a kind of work which is by its very nature impersonal, and at the same time to judge others and give out malicious criticism, would very simply make one guilty of the worst form of hypocrisy. In times like these, nobody will be surprised that like a thief the time of punishment for such a vile and contradictory attitude may suddenly appear. But if I have to emphasize this point in order to be comprehensive, I also know that this matter is not a concern for those who are on the path to illumination. They have, by the very nature of their quest, chosen to improve themselves in order to go forward to the mastery of life by first mastering themselves.

A traditional movement must fulfil its great mission in the service of humanity, and, in order to retain its effectiveness in society, must maintain the integrity and purity of its principles, intervening with vigor and security if any attempt is made to inject into it that which does not correspond to its nature and purpose. The responsibility of those charged with guaranteeing the purity of the program is heavy and essential to success, because its effectiveness is in large part determined by their knowledge of what is at stake. It is this responsibility that each seeker in this final age must assume equally. Vigilance is necessary in order to preserve the traditional ideas in all their purity and power. The ego, source of pride and error, is the danger, even if it seems to be defending certain principles and thereby becoming fanatic and sectarian. Detachment, impersonality, and humility are the rule and duty. I will come back to this important point in a later letter because it is basic to our work. I have referred to it again today because it is a point that serves as the place where all forces of good come together.

My wish, dear friends, is that you reflect over the contents of this letter. Books and articles appear everyday using these great themes to make money, and written to please a public that is confused when faced with the truth. The result is works of imagination whose exaggerations and errors are clear to those who know. Such vain pieces of writing can only have a bad effect if their ideas are accepted as they are presented. They are contrary to the principle of action and positive thought. For the individual their result would be resignation, fear, and inefficiency. Curiosity forces people to want to know at any price, and consequently to accept anything as truth, no matter what. A true seeker, if he remains eager to learn, holds onto logic and the judgement of common sense at all times. Otherwise he would be just a dreamer, a victim of any illusions. In regard to the subjects we have examined in this letter, it is better to hold to the great directions that the past has been able to give us, or that the present can confirm as real. Our understanding of final things is but a function of a train of different circumstances, the purpose of which goes quite beyond humankind. But beyond further developments and opportunities, permanence endures, and at that level human cooperation is possible, desirable and wished for. If this letter goes a little toward making you understand this message, its purpose has been attained.

In the next *Letter from Nowhere* I'll take a different subject that I hope will hold your interest and also stimulate your thinking.

Until then, my dear friends, I remain in the bonds of fellowship,

                        Very sincerely yours,
                        Raymond Bernard

2

APRIL 1977

Kamal Joumblatt, Grand Master of the Druzes

Dear Friends,

A man is dead—assassinated—and this man was my friend, my brother. I knew him better than anyone, and more than anyone, I loved him. I can't imagine not telling you, my friends, what he was and what he truly represented. Up until the fatal hour that interrupted his exceptional destiny, this man was misunderstood, betrayed, and despised. His words and actions, falsely reported or reported out of context, or even completely made up, caused many people to hate him. Their hatred toward this exceptional man prevented them from knowing his real personality. We know that nobody enters into politics without the sudden appearance, somehow, of hostility, but not many outsiders, who are not involved in public life and who are only spectators and witnesses would have the good sense, in the absence of factual information, not to judge a public figure! For how did they feel in the depths of their hearts, those whose judgements were formed solely on the basis of press reports, when this same press, reporting on the death of Kamal Joumblatt, insisted on his exceptional mysticism and the deep spiritual value of the man who was otherwise described as The Very Wise Grand Master of the Druzes?

Kamal Joumblatt's political options were seldom the object of his conversations with me. At least, they were never the reasons for our talks, and when I asked him to clarify something he said in regard to them, he dismissed them and returned to our major themes that were certainly infinitely more elevated and more vast than his political role in a small part of the world.

Most certainly, never in my life have I remained indifferent to the events that affect humankind. Every time I have had the chance to intervene constructively during meetings in many countries at a very high level, although always on a private level, I have been able to do this with recommendations and advice. I have helped redress wrongs, and for humanitarian purposes I have helped change deplorable conditions and tried to promote justice and happiness. I must admit that such actions on my part have brought about successful changes only when my clients had some real power, and such is not always the case, because the impressive titles given to some public figures often mean very little compared with the possibilities one would expect.

Why should the events in Lebanon not have moved me deeply? We have a lot of friends there among the different political and religious factions that make up that country. They are all equally dear to me, and I cannot choose among them. I have suffered with all of them, rather like a father whose children have broken his heart, and more like a brother whose brothers have shattered his dreams with their bloody feuds. Yet in all of this none of them opposed to Kamal Joumblatt had ever reproached me for my close friendship with him, even during the worst times of battle. They all knew that our friendship was something else, and they certainly felt that public words and acts often conceal other motives. He told me that what he wanted was a country not organized along religious lines, a non-confessional country. I am not much of a judge in such matters, but I had to ask him whether that would not be the best solution for the Lebanese crisis, since the use of force had not been able to solve it. I told him that it was only necessary to look at what was happening elsewhere in the world, for example, in Ireland, where two Christian communities were tearing themselves apart, even if the religious question was just a pretext. In any case, if some day soon or far in the future the political make-up were no longer determined by religious factions, and a new constitution assured a secular state, wouldn't Kamal Joumblatt be seen as the one who foretold it and helped prepare the way? Furthermore, it is false to maintain that he was hostile to the existence of Israel as a state. I don't know what has been said and written on this subject and I ignore what he reportedly said publicly on the matter. But I refuse to ignore what he told me personally, and that is that he surely did not want Israel deleted from the map of the world. Finally, if you would like to reproach Kamal Joumblatt for his position in favor of the Palestinian cause, have you really thought about the appalling situation of those people?

We generally believe that the Palestinians are all Moslems. I believed this too until one day, some months before the disaster, I was given special permission to visit their camps in Beirut where I witnessed firsthand the misery of people displaced from their traditional homes. I learned from my driver and from my guide that some Palestinians are Christians just as they are, the proportion of religions being the same throughout the region. Kamal Joumblatt himself was not a Moslem. He was a Druze. Consequently he was not defending members of his own religion in supporting the Palestinians. Knowing him very well, I can say that he was by his very nature drawn to the side of unhappy people. This being the case, who could blame him in the least? In no way can he be blamed for the presence of the Palestinians in Lebanon. The authorities in power are to blame for this sad fact. The legendary and exemplary hospitality of the Lebanese people must be recognized in this regard. But it is easy to see that after years and years the presence of these strangers has grown to be badly resented among the Lebanese. For surely this hospitable country with such a great heart hopes to put itself back together as it was. For how long can anyone play host to strangers? And probably the Lebanese did not think that the Palestinians would stay so long. To make the matter worse, is it not possible that the Palestinians, living together surrounded by other people, will rebel against those who took them in? The younger generation of Palestinians will not be able to see their situation the way their elders did. The more they try to escape from their refugee status and better themselves, the more they will irritate and cause trouble for the community that shelters them.

To all this we must add the Palestinian war against Israel as a huge problem, and the guilty indifference of the whole world. We begin to see the necessity of giving the unfortunate Palestinians a homeland. We had better think about it long and hard before the exasperation of two implacable groups creates a blood bath of which innocent people will be the victims. It is my opinion that the essential responsibility for this tragic Palestinian business lies with the whole world. We have got to face up to the problems caused by one nation acting against another. We have hidden our faces and allowed the horror to proceed. Is it really necessary that the worst should happen? Should we simply acquiesce in the face of destruction? Keeping the status quo is not a final solution when it depends on a divisive and fractured community. If to govern is to anticipate events, it is certain that those responsible around the world for the sorry state of Lebanon are really wretched governors (couldn't we say as much about other situations?)

Have I committed a political act in giving out these thoughts? I don't know, but if I am judged to have done so I accept the judgement. After all, to a mystic, nothing that is human can be foreign, and if to express an opinion about a given situation is to adopt a political position, I won't deny that I have done so. Not being a fanatic and remaining open to all points of view, even those opposed to my own, I don't assume that my thinking is the most authoritative.

Kamal Joumblatt was the co-founder (with another of my friends, who didn't share his ideas, and so dropped out) of the Lebanese Progressive Party. The term progressive being significant elsewhere, he was considered a leftist everywhere. I can't freely accept the word left as signifying a political vision of things. Left in relation to what? This designation is supposed to stand for ideas that are advanced, compared with the actual state of affairs. However, ideas are linked together. They advance on their own or by force. If we describe this motion as going from right to left, then while the ideas advance it is evident that there no longer exists, strictly speaking, a right. However, we have to take existing terminology into account and there is no doubt that in regard to special interests and the power of money Kamal Joumblatt was progressive. He did not merely extol ideas, he lived them, for example by giving away a large part of his lands. In other words, he did not just talk about the redistribution of property. He put his ideas into practice. Being his close friend and confidant, I can assure you that his progressivism was the exoteric manifestation of his asceticism, or more precisely, of the mysticism which was his life. Kamal Joumblatt may have appeared under different, even contradictory facets to many. The man I knew, however, was unique and complete, his mystical beliefs explaining his seeming excesses of language and attitude. If people had paid careful attention to him and followed him, it is possible that sooner or later his country would have entered a new era of development. Idealism projects itself into the future, beyond current external conditions. What Kamal had in mind as an ideal might or might not have come to pass. In his conversations with me, I observed that he was often much more than an idealist. They called him a dreamer, a visionary, even a prophet, and like all prophets his mind was on another level. Could he have been understood? The facts show that he was not.

After this long digression, I want to tell you about my private and friendly relations with Prince Kamal Joumblatt. I had no other intention when I started writing this letter, but thinking involves all sorts of diversions that being expressed may become important, so I won't suppress the ideas that come to me.

It is time, however, to get back to my main intention. As I relive this story through these few pages, my absent friend will come back to life for me. It is in opening my memory and my heart that I will get my reward—to be again as before with my departed friend.

My first encounter with Kamal Joumblatt occurred at the end of February, 1967. Returning from a visit to Israel and Jordan, I was due to stop in Beirut. When I was in Israel the authorities did not stamp a visa in my passport because I was going to visit Arab countries. I would have been refused entry into Jordan and Lebanon if even a single Israeli mark were in my passport. In spite of this, and in order to avoid going through the customs and immigration office, the chief lawyer Fouad Rizk, who was then Minister of Justice, showed the goodwill and courtesy to pick me up at the airplane, making my entry into Lebanon very easy.

It was while talking with Fouad Rizk about the deep interest that the Druze people inspired in me that I first got the idea of meeting Kamal Joumblatt. He and Fouad Rizk were intimate friends, even though they didn't agree on political matters, and he suggested that he could set up an interview at his house with Joumblatt, which I eagerly accepted. I was then told that Kamal Joumblatt was not in the habit of following any protocol, and I should not be astonished or offended if after a few minutes Joumblatt got up and left the room. That would simply mean that he didn't want anything to do with me. Anyway, if that were to happen, it wouldn't bother me. I am too respectful of the freedom and feelings of others, at all times and in all circumstances, to be put off by any bad impression I might make on them. The old proverb is true: you can't please everyone. I have never known it to be otherwise in the manifested world, where the law of polarity always works everywhere. Thus if anyone or anything seems unattractive in any way, this does not mean that the love of people and things cannot be universal. The mistake lies only in the words we use. So, no one ought to say: I don't like such a person or such a thing. It would be more precise to say: This person or this thing does not attract me, which is quite different from not liking. Certainly, I would have regretted it if a current of sympathy had not been established between the two of us. At that time I considered him to be the only way for me to have access to the heart of the Druze people, or rather to their secret wisdom, if that were possible and permissible. I wasn't even thinking about friendship with the prince.

The interview came about one evening a few days after I arrived in Beirut. It lasted nearly two hours! I can still see the smile of satisfaction on Rizk's face. After Joumblatt had left, he said: You won. In fact it was much more than that. From our first words together a real communion was established between the prince and me. After breaking the ice, I felt it was necessary for me to explain my own experiences on the initiatory path to him. This I did in precise terms at great length. Kamal Joumblatt listened to me without ever interrupting me. He sat by my side, leaning back on the couch, his hands crossed on his knees in a striking attitude of grandeur and nobility. He was dressed in a dark suit, a white shirt and black tie. He always dressed like that over the years, and I wasn't surprised when the press, in reporting his assassination, alluded to his shabby suit. He didn't seem to actually pay any attention to grooming and external appearances. He didn't need to. His personality made you forget or ignore the rest.

When I was finished telling him about my quest, I abruptly asked him a question about the Druzes, showing my intense interest in them. Joumblatt answered me circumspectly, but in an exhaustive way, covering all the points he felt he could. I got the feeling, however, that he would really have to confer with others before telling me more about the wisdom of the Initiated

Druzes. Knowing full well the law of Initiation, I assured him of my discretion. He told me enough, in spite of the circumstances, to enable me to write shortly thereafter my study entitled *A Secret Order: the Druzes*. Of course, sworn to secrecy about the revelation and details that he gave me, and agreeing that a veil of silence must always cover them, I have honored his request. His request for secrecy, moreover, only covered certain specifically defined kinds of knowledge and experience that are quite glorious. The request did not pertain to many other subjects that I have felt free to refer to on many occasions, subjects that are immensely interesting to seekers and mystics.

It was in the course of this same interview that Joumblatt brought up the question of the new *Mahdi* that the Druzes are awaiting, the Mahdi being for them a divine incarnation that happens every hundred years. He let me know in no uncertain terms that, taking the cycles into account, the new Mahdi would have a universal mission, going far beyond the Druzes alone. Later we seldom spoke about this subject, Joumblatt saying briefly that out of respect and in order to prevent any interference we should not talk about it. I finally learned from him that the problem had to do with the vehicle of the instructor. The physical body did not seem adapted for the mission. In such a situation one has to know when to be silent, and so I did not press him further, the best attitude being to remain ready, and to wait and see.

Our first conversation and several others that followed took place for the most part in English. I had been told that Joumblatt preferred to express himself in that language. I didn't know whether he spoke French. I figured that he had some personal or traditional reasons for his choice of language. It was at a later meeting that he hesitated over an English word and substituted the French equivalent. I saw immediately that he had a perfect knowledge of French. Having shown that he could speak French (admirable French, I must say), he translated what he had said into English and insisted that from then on we speak no other language. He certainly made a decision and a choice at that point. In following years I heard him speak French on radio and television, and just after he insisted on speaking English with me I watched him on a French television program that was about him. In all this he spoke French. I wonder whether in order to do that he had to get over a bias or prejudice. Would it be presumptuous on my part to say that our friendship had something to do with his decision to speak English with me? Knowing my friend, I don't think so. Moreover, after thinking about it, his motive wasn't important. What was important was that our conversations were made easier and more intimate. I remember how, when he needed a little time to think about his response to a delicate question, he would pretend to ask for the question to be repeated by saying What? in a drawn-out, musical voice. It was a useless What? because he always answered the question immediately. In relating this fact I can hear Joumblatt's What?, and the voice takes me far away into spheres where the moment melts into universal permanence.

I met with Joumblatt several times in Paris. He came often to make official or discrete contacts, and sometimes he came simply to converse with me over dinner. He would phone me, we would meet, and the next day he would go home. A meal with him was always frugal, really only a pretext. I remember a dinner in the restaurant of the Grand Hotel in Paris, and the astonished look on the face of the head waiter when he ordered two plates of spaghetti with butter and a bottle of mineral water! He was so astonished that he dropped the big, luxurious menu that he was holding.

A few years ago in Cairo I learned from a Lebanese friend that Kamal Joumblatt was there at the same time. I wanted to make contact with him to let him know that I was there. He was staying at the Sheraton. I was at the Hotel Meridien. There by the Nile we had a chat on the phone, and then he came to visit me. I told him that the next month I would be in Beirut and if he was willing I would like to meet, finally, some Druze Sages, some of the Learned Ones who possess the Great Knowledge. He asked me to ask him again when I got to Beirut. It was during that interview that he gave me his views of Israel. I learned in particular that the Druzes of Israel are the only non-Jews that the Israelis accept in their army, and whom they look up to. In effect, the Druzes observe the traditional, secular rule of respecting the laws of the country where they live. Here is another fact that ought to make the political pundits think again. Wouldn't it have taken just a single word from Kamal Joumblatt for things to go differently? His people live in several countries, but he himself, the chief, was bound by the law of tradition which transcends the limitations of the individual and the ego. What kind of power could any Order wield, if its members lived in several countries and ignored the laws of those countries while observing only its law? Every traditional rule has a solid foundation for the one who knows how to go beyond the limits of the puny self and extend his vision to vaster horizons.

I found it difficult to reach Kamal Joumblatt in Beirut. I finally did and he phoned me. I was at the Hotel Phoenicia and he came to see me there. I was seated in the big lobby when he came in. Seeing him walking toward the desk where several people were waiting, instead of asking the concierge to speak to him, I walked rapidly toward him. That's when I had a new experience of the power and cohesion of a secret order like the Druzes. Naturally, some Druzes worked at the hotel, some at the desk, others in the restaurant and bar. The arrival of Kamal Joumblatt among them had the effect of a lit trail of gunpowder. And so as we walked side by side toward the elevator, we were surrounded by young people apparently occupied with doing other things, not paying any attention to us, but in reality forming a shield around us. When the door opened, a young man wearing a red jacket, who should have been in the bar, came out of nowhere and took possession of the elevator where he stood smiling at us. I don't know how this happened because we were at the back of the crowd. Then Joumblatt and I found ourselves alone in the elevator watched with respect and affection by the young man with smiling eyes. He looked at Joumblatt with devotion. "That's Druzes for you!" Joumblatt said simply. Sometime later, having ordered a drink for my friend, I saw the same waiter, bewildered to see the prince there, waiting silently, trying to figure out how to approach the prince without embarrassing himself. At this point, I turned to my friend and murmured, "Still a Druze, isn't he?"

It was a Wednesday. After Joumblatt had told me about his progress on the path of mysticism, he spoke at length about the differences between the Shir and the Invisible Company. This is all I can tell you about this matter for those who can understand. Afterwards, I recall that I told him about my own journey on this path. He is one of the few with whom I have shared secrets that I feel I do not have the right, for many reasons, to reveal. Then, having shared our usual experience of spiritual communion, I reminded him of the request I had made in Cairo. Could I meet some Druze Sages this time? I had to go home on Sunday and so I had three days left. "It will be difficult to get them all together," Kamal said, "Perhaps two or three. It shouldn't be any problem. Which day is convenient for you?" We finally chose Saturday. The minister Fouad Rizk would drive me to the prince's castle at Mokhtara in the Druze mountains.

A little early on Saturday Fouad Rizk came to my hotel and we left. Riding along I realized that I had forgotten to bring my identification papers, but I declined Fouad's friendly offer to go back to get them. It was some months before the great, bloody explosion, and check points had been set up by the army on all the roads leaving Beirut and at some spots in the city. But we were not stopped and our trip of just over an hour occurred without incident.

I can see in my mind's eye the mountain roads, savage, uneven and barren, but spellbinding in their loneliness. I can see the quaint villages perched on the flanks of rugged mountains that seemed to be welcoming me. I can see the villagers' faces lit up with fraternal smiles, while we were haphazardly climbing the steep slopes.

I see again the sudden appearance of the castle as we rounded a turn in the road, a tiny place that fell from view as we climbed up the gorge.

The car entered the courtyard through the open gate and stopped. Two men walked toward us. As I would later learn, one was Kamal's driver, the other his bodyguard. Later they would both die with their master. I wept for them too, for although I knew them only briefly, I appreciated their uprightness, their absolute loyalty to the death, and I loved them. They were studying us courteously but firmly when suddenly Kamal appeared. They were certain that we were the ones they were waiting for, and being cordial they withdrew, having accepted us like one of their own. Kamal smiled a big smile. What an event for me! I always found him happy, but he seldom smiled, though he was always happy and relaxed when we met. I sometimes thought that a Druze prince, even a progressive one, would have to appear reserved and serious because of his training and environment. But his background did not affect the comradeship and boundless friendship that he displayed to a few lucky people.

Talking all the while, we walked toward the castle. It had been suggested to me several times that I should not go through a door ahead of my host. It was a custom that the prince himself must not fail to observe, a custom that resulted in an amusing scene. I waited in front of the door for him to go in, and he waited for me to go in. I glanced quickly at Rizk. He seemed as confused as I. And while we were waiting for each other to make up our minds, Kamal and I exchanged some words that cannot be repeated until he understood and, giving me a little shove, he made me step across the sill first, murmuring "You are my friend!" I felt that this gesture was not an honor, that would be vanity, but a sign of affection, and I was moved.

Two or three Druze Sages, he had said. I supposed that they would arrive later. Kamal pointed to a door on the left, and it opened. I went in, and a sudden, brutal, mystical emotion descended on me like a hurricane of light. It bowled me over, shattering my being into a myriad selves until finally, at a solar level, I was again unified with a different, superior personality, the one I am familiar with and which I put on in the solitude of my private chapel, or in the course of certain ceremonies, or in the course of certain encounters. At these times, the receptivity of others reaches beyond the physical aspect and its useful, dark, protective cloak, and allows the Master to speak in me or through me. They were there, the Druze Sages, in the blue vibration of a large blue room, on the walls of which were hung, here and there, framed parchments in Arabic writing. They were there, not two, not three, not ten, but more than twenty. They had ceased whatever they were doing to obey the call from their Grand Master. Some came from afar, from Syria, which meant one or two nights of travel. They were there, dressed in their traditional garb, black in color, tight trousers and vests, with white caps on their heads. All but one had long, curly beards. But it was especially their eyes that astonished me. Intense or calm, they were eyes of light. One by one I greeted them, my gaze melting into theirs, and soon there grew among us an all-powerful feeling of friendship, of welcome, as if I were being dubbed a knight. Yes, it was at that moment when I was accepted that I believe I crossed the high threshold, something that the Initiated Druzes generally never allow strangers to do. Yes, these Initiated Druzes were Sages in every sense of this term, for it was in that first contact that we said everything to each other.

As I took my seat among them, Kamal on my left and Rizk on my right, the prince himself served as my interpreter. Although we had said everything to each other simply by looking at one another, now, without stopping our communion, we had to give our thoughts words and share our knowledge. Thus we spoke for nearly two hours, they answering my questions, to verify the similarities between the great traditions and the ancestral, secular convictions of the Druzes at each stage.

How I would have loved to have had other seekers with me at that meeting! If they had been there, their certainty would have been reinforced by it. The uniformity of traditions developing distinctly and in different forms, practically without any prior contact outside of that which I had the privilege to be able to establish, would have astonished them. Some of them would have been helped to overcome the inhibitions caused by their supposedly scientific educations, educations that in fact were restricted and dominated by materialistic concepts, or supposedly religious educations that were in reality deformed by an intolerant fanaticism. They would have better understood the value of Western initiatory training (and the power of the techniques included in it). Certainly, that which I got from the assembly of Druze Sages was not only a confirmation of the teachings and practices of our own Western tradition. There were a lot of other things that I can't write or talk about, but which I was authorized to sow here and there like separate seeds in writings and talks. The foresight of those Sages was so great that they gave me a mandate to give this knowledge to certain people so that it would never be lost since the cosmic order of things wants their spiritual and mystical aspirations to go in the same direction as mine in order to demonstrate, if need be, that chance doesn't exist in any field when it is a matter of service and initiation.

There is, however, one fact that I will relate to you. It is somewhat like another one that I knew about, but in the realm of mysticism everything is more or less in agreement, and this fact will interest you. As you doubtless know, and as I have written elsewhere, the Druzes believe in reincarnation, and not only do they believe in it, it is the very foundation of their belief. This conviction is shared by all the Druze people, not only the Sages and the Initiated. Knowing that, toward the end of our meeting, I asked whether any members of that august assembly could remember his last incarnation. They all smiled, as if to suggest that my question seemed infantile to them and that everyone knew what there was to be known on that subject. Then they spoke among themselves, and finally they turned to a beardless Sage, as if he had been designated to speak. This Sage, I later learned, lived in Venezuela, where he was engaged in important business. Returning to Lebanon to steep himself in the life of pure wisdom that his initiated brothers led, he heard Kamal's appeal, and so he was among us that day. Here is a resume of his story:

At the beginning of this century, France was engaged in a war against the Druzes. I was in the mountains behind a big rock. At a certain moment, I half-way stood up to fire my rifle. A bullet hit me and I fell down dead. Some years later in my present life—I must have been five or six years old—I suddenly understood that I had another family, and this impression was so strong that my present family, the one I was born into, seemed nearly strangers to me. I spoke about this matter with my relatives, giving them all the details that little by little were coming into my memory. Being good Druzes, like everybody they knew all about the doctrine of reincarnation. They listened to me carefully, questioning me and helping me to remember. My need to see my old family again grew more and more demanding. My parents started looking into the matter, using the information I gave them. They were very rich. I was their only son. My memories were very precise, so they didn't have to look very long. My former family was located. They were very poor. I was driven to the outskirts of the village. The clouds in my memory blew away. I walked directly to what had been my home in my former life. I recognized everybody related to me, and I brusquely asked them where was my uncle who used to live with us in that house. I even remembered his name! My former family accepted me right off, and since I couldn't bear to live away from them, my father (the one in my present life) bought some land near my old house, and that's where I grew up, my parents taking care of my former relatives. When I grew up, I took care of them. And I still do today.

Most of us would find such a tale so unbelievable that we would prefer to say that it had its origin in a very fertile imagination. If mysticism were not an integral part of my existence, it is evident that as a good Westerner imbued with materialistic science, and skeptical by nature, I should deny any such possibility or anything that transcends the shabby knowledge of my science with the haughty disdain of my closed mind. But the fact is that I feel myself attracted to that which is beyond human limitations, and that is what justifies my presence in these places. Furthermore, everyone who spoke radiated with such certainty and peace, their words being so calm and true, that I did not doubt for a single moment. The whole group received that testimony with confidence and respect. On no face was there a smirk of doubt. Every one of them, no doubt, was reminded of what he knew about his own past.

Among the Initiated Sages, several of them gained my attention. They were among the others, but they did not speak, and I felt that they must comprise a group with an elevated, secret function. Two among them particularly attracted me, and of the two, one somewhat more than the other. I visualized a mental question: Are you the Master? and I looked at him. Leaning on his cane, his whole being beaming with love and goodwill, he smiled—and what a smile!—and slowly, his eyes on mine, he winked twice. When we parted, I kissed his hand in respect, and still smiling, he gathered me in his arms and gave me his blessing. These were unforgettable moments whose memory makes me relive them again!

The other Sage was a short fellow. His long and wide beard framed a thin face with vibrant, piercing eyes. His gnarled body seemed stuck to the bench he was sitting on. He was crippled, and so immobile. I don't know why he looked like a schoolmaster to me. Anyway, that's what I called him to myself, and you will see later on that I wasn't entirely wrong.

Our meeting over, I supposed that we were going to part. A few of the Sages left us walking in the gardens around the castle.

But it wasn't time for me to leave. A meal, or rather I should say a communion, was waiting for us. A fraternal lunch brought us together in the great dining hall of the castle in Mokhtara. Fouad Rizk told me it was the first time in the history of the Druze people that a stranger had shared a meal with the Initiated. I don't feel any pride about it. On the contrary, I feel an overwhelming sense of humility and indebtedness. The meal was a true communion, and the vegetarian food was succulent, both cooked and raw, with fruit in abundance, everything served by silent waiters who were discreet and efficient. Basically the meal was a pretext to be together again, united in spirit by the symbol of a meal in common. And when it was over, I had a feeling that a new, strong and powerful link had just been forged between me and my hosts, and certainly between the spiritual forces that, having a common origin, were indivisible in their eternal essence. And then the Sages departed, dignified, silent, smiling, radiant, carrying with them our exchange of looks and feelings.

Fouad Rizk left us. He had wanted me to go in his car, and he was quite insistent. But Kamal offered me the use of his, and something made me believe that he wanted to say a few more words to me. Rizk spoke briefly with his driver; he seemed to be quite preoccupied. I wouldn't understand this until much later on the 16th of March, 1977, when I learned about the outrage perpetrated against Kamal not far from where we were. His green Mercedes was well known, and so were his driver and his bodyguard, under whose feet in the front seat there was a machine gun that he did not show me until we arrived back in Beirut. The Mercedes was saluted by drivers of other cars and pedestrians. The army didn't control that car. One day it would become a funeral pyre.

As soon as Rizk had left, Kamal asked for his car. At that moment, the Sage that I had named for myself the schoolmaster came toward us. While the car was being brought up the steep and barely passable road to the castle, the schoolmaster and I engaged in conversation, with Kamal interpreting and adding a judicious comment occasionally. We spoke about doctrine again, in order to verify further the extraordinary concordance between Druze wisdom and the tenets of other traditions. This agreement is so strong, even in minor details, that at one point Kamal exclaimed "This similarity signifies unity and truth. It is proof for you and for us too. The groups of people are different: the wisdom and the message are one."

Finally we got to where we were going. The countryside was bare. It was very rocky with hardly any vegetation. We drove up to a plain building. I was surprised by it because it wasn't visible until we came upon it. It was built on a summit on the side of the mountain, surrounded on all sides by steep mountain valleys that seemed infinitely deep. In the distance and well below us we could barely see the castle of Mokhtara. Could this building be a watch tower? A door opened and a young Druze came out. He would be our guide. We had hardly entered when I began to understand, and Kamal confirmed what I thought. We were in the secret school of the Druze, in the house of initiation. My impression had not tricked me; the Sage really was a schoolmaster, but the master of a different school, a school beyond time, a school of high and pure wisdom. That building had been constructed on a site where a Druze hermit, who had achieved the great liberation, had lived. With respect and emotion, we went into the tiny grotto where he had stayed. There where he had meditated, gathering ourselves together, we had a few moments of overwhelming communion. Of course, I can't tell you what I saw and heard in that place of secrecy and wisdom. I am bound to silence. I can tell you, however, that I met young Druze disciples who had heard and felt the call. Having abandoned their daily affairs, they were there to prepare themselves, to learn and become familiar with the initiation before returning to the outside world to practice a profession like all the Druzes, if only the traditional and respected profession of farming, without ever ceasing in their interior quest. That building reminded me of others I had known. The mystical intensity was the same. The fact that such exalted places can secretly carry on their work amid a troubled world gives us reason to hope and have confidence... Before leaving, my hosts and I shared a frugal lunch, feeling the importance of this exchange very strongly, remembering that the cenacle has always represented a true rite that notably the Essenes practiced with fervor... While returning to Mokhtara, I turned several times to try to catch a glimpse of the building, but it melted into the grey mass of the mountain and it was impossible to make it out. It was sufficient to know that it was there, to remember its existence. The schoolmaster went with us to the castle. He held my hand for a long time, then he left, lively, ageless, to go about his business. Dear schoolmaster, how often have my thoughts gone to you in your mountains, in your secret building, among those whom you teach?

Upon our return Kamal had me visit his home. He showed me into rooms that only he and his family were allowed to enter. With characteristic humility he explained the pictures to me, identifying the portraits of his princely ancestors, and giving me time to contemplate those whom I was particularly drawn to. The castle was then undergoing extensive repairs. I was certain, and I was later proven right, that Kamal did not undertake the restoration for himself, but rather out of respect for his lineage and for the love of his people. At that point, his calm face suddenly filled with emotion. "Come," he said, "we are going to my secret retreat."

We went up the stairs of a nearby building, and as we went up, everything grew poorer and simpler, displaying a particular austerity. The door that my friend opened gave onto a relatively small room covered with carpets. In one corner there was a couch, a sort of low pallet. That was where, at the castle of Mokhtara, Prince Kamal Joumblatt, the Very Wise Grand Master of the Druzes, reposed near a simple altar, also down near the floor. There, before a portrait, burned a votive lamp, and some incense. The portrait was that of Kamal's Hindu Guru, the man he chose and who had accepted him. Sri Atmananda of Trivandrum had helped him up the last steps toward divine Realization and to the level of synthesis from which there is no return. Since there are in India several other persons and Sanyasins of different orders known under the name Atmananda, it is necessary to specify Trivandrum as the name of the Sat-Guru of whom we speak. "My Master is no more," Kamal whispered to me, "insofar as he has left his human appearance, but every day I identify more and more with him."

It was there in that sacred ambience that Kamal gave me final revelations about his mystical and spiritual experiences. That was when I got to know him totally as a whole person, and that was when, in listening to him and seeing him, I would understand the real motives behind his acts, the why of his political, social and human ideas, and the reasons for certain of his public declarations. I believe that since that day I should even have been able to understand also the words attributed to him, which he later let me hear, that he had never said, or at least that he would not have said. His mistake (if it was a mistake) had been to act and to express himself on the level he had achieved personally on the Path of Evolution, and with the incommunicable understanding that such heights represent, without paying attention to the fact that most people could not understand him. But what else could he have done? What for others was a final goal was an integral part of Kamal: action and service without any thought or consideration of the outcome of the action and service. Such an attitude toward life could be taken as eccentricity or pride. It could be judged utopian, and one with such an attitude could be taken as a dreamer in certain circumstances, or as an ogre in other cases. That didn't bother Kamal Joumblatt any more than it would have bothered whoever had achieved such heights of realized consciousness. Dharma, duty, in the absolute sense of the term, is at that stage of evolution the only valid motive. Even more, the Initiated has become the Dharma itself.

According to the Western way of thinking, it would appear astonishing and perhaps delusive that Kamal Joumblatt, imbued with the great wisdom of the Druzes and having received the highest initiations in his own tradition, would apparently need a personal guru to perfect his knowledge. An Oriental mystic would not perceive any such problem, since for him there is no separation or split among those who search for God. Ramakrishna, for example, having achieved absolute liberation, voluntarily went back to practice the spiritual exercises of various religions. He followed the ways of Christianity and Islam, among others. He didn't have to do this, but in so doing he extended his knowledge and experience of the perceived and the manifested in order to better serve and enlighten others. It is evident that for those who are still on the Path, but who have not reached a certain level of understanding, to do so would be a dangerous, even fatal, waste of psychic energy. In order to climb the mountain of illumination, a path that has been followed by crowds of others, that has had each segment recognized and marked out over the course of time by innumerable seekers, is the surest and most efficient way to get to the end. Once there, no danger to consciousness can arise, and you can improve your mind through ways that are new to you. This you should do always with a view toward helping those who are still seeking. Besides, the accomplishment is not the end of the evolution. It is *an* end, and this is what permits great illumined ones to affirm that even the most advanced remain mere beginners. The reef on which you can founder, as a matter of fact, is to suppose that, just because you have climbed one summit among the summits, everything is accomplished. This is a barrier that can make you take a detour and look outside for what you, like every human being, have in yourself. Actually, the point is not to look outside yourself, but to discover it inside yourself.

Kamal Joumblatt, in his determination and effort to go beyond, had chosen a path to enlarge his consciousness based on the Druze Initiation that he had completed. This path was the pure Jnana-Yoga, that is to say, absolute Knowledge—a knowledge that cannot be moderated by Bhakti-Yoga, otherwise called *of Devotion*. Jnana-Yoga is a way, exclusive in itself, that accepts no compromise. Consequently, it may appear dry and rigorous to ordinary people because it is so barren. It is a pure monism (Advaita), a perfect and integral accomplishment of Unity. In reality, it contains all the paths, even Bhakti-Yoga, because it is more than a consecration—it is a fusion, an absorption in the All, and that does not mean that the Individual is separate from the *Maya,* otherwise called the illusion of the created. He continues more intensely than ever to participate in the *lila* or the game of the world, but without the Self, the witness, being affected by it. The Self, having become the All, is a beacon of light that shines across the spirit of the Jnanin through the manifested to which react those who have been reached by it in order for the divine work to be accomplished, and for the scheme of things to unfold in the foreseen way. Jnana-Yoga requires, at the beginning, enough intellect to understand it, then the training of the intellect, and finally the abandonment of that very intellect in Unity. There is not a more difficult path, and it can only be the path of one who is fulfilled, because it includes for other people the danger of confusing the means with the end, and the consequences could be incalculable.

Kamal gave me three books to help me better understand his quest, and to share it sympathetically. They were all in English. The first is a collection of basic aphorisms by his guru, entitled *Spiritual Discourses of Sri Atmananda* (of Trivandrum, 1950-1959). The second is entitled *Atmanandopanishat,* the third *Rambles in Vedanta,* the latter being a sort of commentary on the Vedanta in general.

I hope that this rapid survey of the mystical life of Kamal Joumblatt will help you understand what is essentially true about him. His detractors claimed that he called himself the reincarnation of Akhenaton. If he had thought that, he would have told me. He never made mention of this claim in all our encounters, even when we were sharing the most intimate mystical knowledge. Of course he held that wise pharaoh in immense veneration, but being a Druze, he also venerated Pythagoras and Plato, among others. It would be incredible for him to have made such a claim to a barely enlightened population. I doubt it very much. Again his words were distorted. It was a way of destroying him as a political force in Lebanon. It wasn't hard to make people believe that he made such claims, and a lot of people believed them, but I did not! Moreover, these stupid rumors were no better than the people who made them up. Their absurdity is obvious.

September, 1976, eight months later, I was in Cairo again. I was told that the newspapers had announced that Kamal Joumblatt was going to visit President Sadat, but nobody knew whether he had arrived yet. The next day I was sitting in the lobby of my hotel, watching the incessant traffic outside the main door. Suddenly, seeing a Mercedes like Kamal's, I thought of him. I turned to my companion and asked him to inquire at the desk whether my friend was, by any chance, staying at the same hotel. He came back in a few minutes to tell me that not only was Kamal staying at the Hilton, his suite was on the same floor as mine! I quickly wrote a note on a piece of hotel stationery and had the concierge put it in Kamal's message box. It stayed there for more than a day. Finally, my companion got the note from the box when he saw Kamal in the lobby surrounded by officials and guards, and gave it to a member of the official party.

The next morning, the telephone rang in my suite. It was him! We chatted for a few minutes, and then he exclaimed, "It's curious, isn't it, that we have run into each other so often in Cairo without planning to!" For him, and for me, it was not curious, for beyond words at a certain level there is no such thing as chance. He wanted to see me. When? But immediately, and a few minutes later he was there at my door with guards protecting him. There we were, together again. In spite of serious political events and grave preoccupations, he was the same old Kamal. I knew we wouldn't have much time together that day. We had a rambling conversation. A confusing feeling came over me. I told him to be careful, to look after himself. But for him, as for me, again those were only words. We both had in mind, as do many others, the fact that the *great departure* is a function of service, that it is fixed in advance, so to speak, and nobody can do anything about it. He told me about the situation in Lebanon in greater detail than he had ever done before. I spoke to him about my friends over there whom I was constantly worried about. I spoke with him about peace, we rose to the usual level of our higher preoccupations where our conversation became silence... communion! Our meeting was not to last very long. Already someone was knocking on the door. I opened it. One of Kamal's secretaries hurried in. It was time for an official visit. He had to leave right away. "I'll see you again before I leave Cairo," my friend said.

Our next meeting happened the next day. Kamal had to leave Cairo sooner than he had planned to, and he sent word that he was waiting for me. I walked to his suite, watched by a vigilant and naturally suspicious guard. Happily, a secretary recognized me and came to get me. The prince and I chatted about this and that, nibbling almonds, with members of his party bustling about. Then he had a long telephone conversation, apparently labored and sad, and I can still see my friend near the telephone on the bed, his left elbow on the bed, the receiver at his right ear. I got up to leave, feeling that it was time, and he hung up. He wanted me to stay but he knew that he had to leave Cairo in a few minutes. I sent for my companion, who wanted to be presented to Kamal and was waiting in the living room. Then Kamal told me that he would be going to Paris soon on official business, and that he wanted to see me then since I would be back home by then. He wrote down my telephone number in his pocket agenda. In Paris, no doubt because of the press of his duties and of my own, we did not get together and didn't even have a phone conversation... Our affectionate handshake in Cairo was the last. Our so long had been a goodbye.

On that morning of Wednesday, the 16th of March, my wife awoke perplexed. She had never met Kamal Joumblatt. She knew only what a place he had in my thoughts and in my heart. But the dream she had just had was strange: Kamal Joumblatt had sent me a telegram to invite me to dinner, and I had declined his invitation. Then he telephoned to tell me that he was in exile, and he renewed his invitation. Again I declined, and my wife pointed out to me that I had better accept, that my friend was in exile and that he was surely waiting for me to show him even greater affection. My wife told several people about her dream because I was away on a long trip. Several hours after my wife's dream the drama occurred.

San Francisco, Wednesday, March 16th, 1977. It was around seven o'clock in the morning, eight hours difference from France. The phone rang. I was told about the assassination of Kamal Joumblatt and the circumstances were explained: the automobile was attacked, the driver and bodyguard were killed too. In a brief instant my memory took me back to the Druze mountains, to the castle of Mokhtara, to an assembly of Sages. I was speechless, my heart broken in the grip of grief. A thought crossed my mind. By San Francisco time, my friend, far away, was still alive. I was informed of my wife's dream. I interpret it like this: Kamal, in the reality of his being, knew what was going to happen. He projected his deep thought toward the place where he knew my home to be. He wanted to tell me. I wasn't there. My wife got the message.

After the short conversation with my wife, I sat motionless, and I lived again in my memory an exceptional friendship. A feeling of deep peace came over me. Separation? What separation? Absence? What absence? Service is never interrupted. Only the means of service, the body, is from time to time given up for another, and that happens when it must and when the greater work demands it. Personalities, beyond the appearance of the visible world, remain united in constant communion. Kamal

Joumblatt is, in this moment of meditation, present here with me. I feel his presence. Even more, I see him.

According to Druze traditions, the reincarnation of the soul is immediate. I have written elsewhere that this is my conviction in regard to really advanced persons, and such are the Initiated Druzes. At the San Francisco airport, at the end of my stay in California, a young crippled person in a wheel chair asked me and my companion for a donation to a religious cause. I hesitated, but my friend responded to this request, and finally I did too, explaining that we were French. A current of sympathy was established. When we had to go, the young woman picked up a big bag, took out a book and offered it to us. It was a magnificent copy of the Bhagavad Gita, a work that Kamal had loved too. Later, reading the introduction, I noticed the reference to a Hindu belief based on ancient Indian doctrines: Death occurs when the new body destined to contain the soul personality is ready to receive it, that is to say, at the moment of the birth of the new body. And there again, I believe, at least for advanced souls, that is what takes place.

Then my thoughts went back to the tragic death of Kamal Joumblatt, and to what went on before. He had felt for a long time that his task in this existence was finished, and so he had decided to completely renounce the world. He was planning to leave Lebanon and go to live in an ashram in India where they keep the teachings of his former guru alive. On the day of the assassination, he had gone from the castle of Mokhtara down to Beirut to wind up some business and make some final preparations. His present mission, as he saw it, had been achieved, his service was needed elsewhere, and everything was ready for him to assume it when the time was right.

Those who direct the evolution of beings and things from on high had convinced him that his present task was over. Their Wisdom and their Immense Compassion are such that even the wisest and most advanced of this world, even those who have figured everything out, do not know, with rare exceptions, when their *great departure* will happen. This departure is for humankind the highest initiation, and to benefit fully at the level of the Self, no one must know when it is going to happen nor what the initiation consists of. It is more or less brief, given the time and space of our world. But that which is known by the soul, even in the case of immediate reincarnation, is so complete and absolute that days, months, and years may be necessary on the physical and human plane to bring about such an experience. Outwardly, the mind, even if it is mastered, remains full of tricks as long as the body is alive. So it is that Wisdom and Compassion keep us ignorant about when and how we must undergo this unavoidable and definitive change. A feeling or premonition that may or may not be useful in some way to the one who must depart or to those who must stay behind may be all that we get. Such is the way things go, following a plan of justice and goodness that is divinely conceived, even though in our insufficiency we can't always understand it, although our human reaction is also a part of our evolution in the world.

So ends the story of an exceptional friendship. And because everything is linked together, recently at a family reunion in Lyon, after I had told my relatives about this friendship, a young cousin of mine told me that during the Napoleonic Era a Druze prince had given his daughter's hand in marriage to a French officer and that she was a descendant of that couple. How I wished I had known this earlier so that I could have mentioned it in conversation with my departed friend. Certainly that would have interested him, but in addition to ties of blood there are those of tradition that unite all those who are advancing toward the light of truth in a great loving family, no matter where they are or what their nationality. And I have the privilege of belonging to this family. These warm ties were strengthened again and again in the outpouring of affection and sympathy that I received from many seekers after the tragic death of Kamal Joumblatt. To all those who showed me their presence and to all those who thought of me if only for a moment, my heart answered with a message of love and gratitude. Yes, I must say that my friend was also their friend, and through me he loved them because he was their brother.

Greetings and Peace to you, Prince Kamal Joumblatt, very Wise Grand Master of the Druzes! The Great Work is far from being achieved. You are already preparing yourself for the new task, but now more than ever we are together. Certainly, I loved the cloak that your soul illumined among us. I will love the new one just as much, as soon as I have recognized you through it with the cloak that is mine now or which I will assume one day. But in the final lines of this letter to other friends, permit me to burst into silent tears in front of them at the memory of what you were for me, at the grief of not having you such as you were. These are the tears of one who, in the rhythm of worlds and time, and in the eternity of created Unity, remains your friend, your brother, the one you loved.

I thank you, dear friends, for the kind reception you have shown toward the *Letters from Nowhere*. They have allowed me to tell you about this man who was my friend, to let you get to know him, and to a certain extent, to defend his memory from the misunderstandings which may have tarnished it. This was not only a duty, the duty of a friend, but a testimonial, because friendship is a privilege. I know how well you have understood that.

Very sincerely yours,
Raymond Bernard

3
AUGUST 1977

Rosicrucian Mystical Experience

Dear Friends,

This third letter will be entirely different from the preceding ones in that the subject it will treat is the Rosicrucians. As a matter of fact, I intend to tell you about the world-wide convention of the A.M.O.R.C. that took place in Paris from the 4th to the 8th of August last year. This event was too important not to be the object of a short treatise, and I'll go about it in my way, not hesitating to tell you some anecdotes that you will find interesting and even amusing. Here and now I can tell you that the next *Letter from Nowhere* and no doubt some others will be about a long trip that I'm about to undertake, and which I will have started by the time you read this letter. I'm leaving on September 20th for India where I'll stay several weeks. I won't be back until some time in November. I'm sure that I'll have much to tell you, and doubtless to confide in you. Later I'll tell you about a trip that I took in August, 1976, to Japan, the Philippines, Thailand, and Pakistan. The people I met there you will certainly find interesting.

I thought that from the beginning of the planning that the world-wide convention would draw two thousand Rosicrucians. Christian Bernard thought that perhaps four thousand would come. We were finally eight thousand. Everybody admired the organization of the welcoming committee that provided the services of the official administration, of the police, the press, radio and television. In all the airports and train stations, hosts wearing green jackets and ties, with white trousers and shirts, along with hostesses wearing orange, whose hats carried the insignia of the world-wide convention—wings surrounding the solar disk—and signs of their function, greeted the officers of the organization and the Rosicrucians who came to the event. Everywhere special stands had been made available to the A.M.O.R.C., and the arriving members were directed to the stands by loudspeakers, where the public could get information about the Order. It was all done with discrete elegance and a lot of dignity. No one will ever forget that exceptional reception. Wherever each Rosicrucian came from, and some came from afar, he was received by his family.

I promised you some anecdotes. Here are two. The first one concerns me. In order to be at the airport to welcome the Imperator of the A.M.O.R.C., Ralph M. Lewis, my wife and I made sure to arrive on Monday the 1st of August. I had to give a press conference on radio and television the next day. So we were the first to have the privilege of being welcomed and driven to the Concorde Lafayette Hotel by a host and hostess. There we were greeted by other hosts and hostesses who were waiting for us. We were surprised and moved by their warm welcome. Our suite was on the thirty-third floor. That evening, very late, having greeted the Imperator and his wife Gladys, who had come by Concorde to show their sympathy with France, we hoped to go peacefully to sleep, but the phone rang several times by mistake. Finally, at three o'clock in the morning, it rang again. Someone spoke to me in English, asking me the number of the suite, and it was right, but then he asked me who I was. Prudently, I answered, "And who are you?" My caller declared "The king of..." (and he gave the name of an oil-rich Arab country). My response was immediate and calm "And I, Sir, am the...king of France! Please excuse me but the Queen and I are sleepy," and I hung up, thinking it all a joke. But I later learned that that king's daughter did live on that floor of the hotel and her father was accustomed to calling her during the night! I hope he finally got in touch with the princess, and I hope especially that he remembered that France is a republic and he didn't wake a king from his sleep. Anyway, kings are all said to be cousins.

The second anecdote has to do with the Grand Master of Brazil, Maria Moura. The hosts and hostesses were waiting for her airplane and supposed that she would be dressed normally. They did not immediately recognize the Grand Master. She walked right by them without being stopped. It was after Maria had gone past the hosts and hostesses with a group of passengers that someone recognized her and shouted "There she is!" and went to greet her. It is true that Maria was dressed casually, in a blouse and blue jeans. They caught her in time. So, the best way of going unobserved in today's world is to wear blue jeans. I think this is true. At least, that is my impression.

Everything was ready! The credentials were collected in an impeccable fashion, and everyone got a souvenir of the big convention along with his accreditation. The auditorium could hold only four thousand people. Each session would have to be repeated. Simultaneous translation would be made in seven languages so that every one would understand everything. I will write here only about the opening ceremony, the closing ceremony and the Grand Master for French-speaking countries because I have some revelations to make on this subject. Moreover, other matters will be covered in Rosicrucian magazines and other publications, for example, mystical demonstrations by the Imperator that can't be described in detail in writing, presentations by the officers of the Order, mystical convocations, shows, etc. What I can tell you should complement what you can probably see and hear. But I believe that the opening and closing of the world-wide convention were so majestic and so important, even if they have been repeated elsewhere, it won't hurt to hear about them again, especially because it is hard to communicate with those who haven't been through it and felt the stunning effects of those solemn moments.

Absolute silence, the lights have been lowered, the conductor raises his baton and Beethoven's Ninth Symphony begins, filling the auditorium with exalting and inspiring vibrations. Slowly the grand curtain goes up. In the center a huge pyramid with steps on its faces. Around it, both left and right, in equal numbers on both sides on platforms a hundred Rosicrucian Colombes (young girls) are standing, holding lighted torches. Beside the Colombes, dressed in white and black stand one hundred singers, both men and women. The group forms a semi-circle around the pyramid, singing in moving harmony. Below the side-steps, facing each side, a Colombe is seated, holding her torch. In the foreground on each side a Colombe is seated before an ornamental bowl where she tends incense during the ceremony.

Suddenly the Colombes, one after the other, walk toward the audience and go down into the auditorium, holding their torches before them. Their slow advance in majesty in the main aisles and around the sides of the immense room is very impressive. Just being there brings an intense mystical emotion. The orchestra during all this, keeps on with the Ninth Symphony, and the Rosicrucian emblem, huge and covering the whole back-drop gradually lights up to the rhythm of the music. Above the disk the letters A.M.O.R.C. are successively lighted up. Then the Rosicrucian cross finally appears, arm by arm, and then the rose. On the right, a Hermetic rosy cross. splendid in its brilliant colors and sublime in its authentic symbols, lights up. Then, in the image of the sun surrounded by the wings an apparition brightens. It is an immense violet triangle pointing down. So, little by little the world-wide convention comes to life, and the soul of the Order is incarnate in it, giving force and vigor to its most sacred symbols. The Colombes, having finished their course around the room, return slowly to their places and sit down. The choir intones the Prelude and the Hymn to Joy. Three specially chosen Colombes gracefully go up the steps of the pyramid. The one who goes up the back side suddenly takes her place at the top. Two other Colombes stand a little below her on either side. Together they represent and show the triangle on the material plane. The spotlights that have slowly brightened the whole scene now focus intensely on the pyramid and the Colombes. The choir sings continuously, with four soloists singing on cue. Then the three Colombes change places, all together. The Colombe at the apex of the pyramid moves down to the lower level, while the other two move up to where she had been, thus reversing the triangle so that it points downward. Having its lower point symbolized by a Colombe, it now is situated on the immaterial plane, the infinite plane. It shows the mystical sense, meaning, and purpose of the convention. The choir is in the last movement of the Ninth Symphony, claiming the joy of the celebrated hymn.

All of the Colombes, in a single movement, rise and raise their torches toward the three Colombes forming the triangle on the infinite plane. Then they sit down. The three Colombes walk slowly down the steps toward the audience. They stand among the choir, the orchestra, and the four soloists just as the Ninth Symphony ends. For a few seconds the audience is silent. Then there is a seemingly endless ovation as the curtain slowly goes down.

The world-wide convention has begun. We have realized our unity. We are a single soul and will remain so until the end of this unique, grandiose ceremony.

I had never in my long life as a mystic attended anything at the same time so beautiful, powerful and symbolic. The audience greeted the Imperator with affectionate applause, and then he delivered his speech and introduced the individuals in charge of the convention. A state of receptivity in all the Rosicrucians present had been created by the sacred mystery that had just unfolded in front of us. And when it was time for the In Memoriam for Dr. H. Spencer Lewis, founder of our Order in its present cycle, who died on August 2nd, 1939, the harmony established among us was nearly materially palpable. From that moment on, the intellectual and mystical work would begin in the subtle links that had been forged among the participants. As I have said, I will deal with this at length elsewhere.

The closing ceremony would be just as majestic, and many tears of emotion were shed by everyone, because, and this was a surprise, the curtain went up, after the music began, on the same scene that we had witnessed at the opening ceremony. But the three Colombes stayed in place while the orchestra and choir performed. It was only toward the end that they reversed the triangle. The lower Colombe took her place at the apex and the other two went down to their places, remaking the triangle on the material plane, since the Rosicrucians, having learned, received and communed together, must return to the material world in the bosom of which they will forge their own evolution. But who, among the thousands of Rosicrucians, was not feeling regret and sadness at seeing the light of the violet triangle slowly go out, and then the letters C.R.O.M.A., and the Hermetic rosy cross, arm by arm, and the central cross, and finally, the rose? When the Colombes had come back down from the pyramid, and in the center the Supreme Colombe stood alone, holding her torch, and the orchestra and the choir were finishing their performance, and the curtain slowly came down, cheers and applause broke out. We were feeling recognition, admiration and love. The Imperator, his wife Gladys, Christian Bernard, myself and the hosts and hostesses gathered together to say goodbyes. There were so many of them! They had worked so hard beyond expectations that their words were filled with such emotion that their "so longs" would remain as a universal, fraternal force...

In telling you about the world-wide convention, I must relive many moments that must have been sublime for a lot of people. These moments had a fundamental element of visualization and meditation. The two ceremonies served very well as a mental representation of the Celestial Sanctum, primarily and most importantly as the focal point of our unity, strength, and acceptance. For a long time that is what they have been for me, and their importance has transcended the context of the convention to take on a mystical dimension on an infinitely heightened and permanent level.

I must now tell you about the new Grand Master for French-speaking countries, and his traditional ritual initiation on August 7th, 1977 at seven-thirty in the morning. He is, of course, my natural son, but in the framework of our Order and in relation to our tradition, all who know us recognize that I have never considered him to be more than a Rosicrucian brother in our work. I recommended him to the Supreme Grand Lodge, and they, having confidence in my judgement, gave me official permission to give him a position at the head office of the Order in France. Then he worked his way up through the several stages of service. At one point in his career, the Grand Lodge elected him to become the Grand Secretary. From then on I have demanded more from him and have been more severe with him than with anyone else.

I can be much more frank and open in a *Letter from Nowhere* than I can in any explanations or writing that I do for the Order in my official capacity. Furthermore, as I pointed out, in these letters I write to you as my friends, and so it goes without saying that I must express myself freely and openly, in sincerity and truth that you feel in your very being. I will consider this subject with you in several ways. To begin with, I must say that I find it impossible to examine anything whatsoever from a point of view that is only circumstantial, material, and human. Every mystic knows that every element of our lives is part of a cosmic whole, and the law of cause and effect being omnipresent, nothing ever happens by chance. Also, I firmly believe in reincarnation, and in its corollary, karma, or the law of compensation. Consequently, my deep conviction is that no soul-personality is ever incarnated by chance. It is born where it must be born in order to pursue its evolution and to fulfil its mission. That is, as a matter of fact, the action of just and omnipresent laws. In the Orient, where belief in reincarnation is accepted, this idea concerning birth is perfectly logical for everyone. In the diverse Oriental sects, religions, and fellowships, it would be unthinkable, even scandalous, for a son not to assume his father's burden when the father decides the time has come. Of course this is nothing new to those who are familiar with Oriental beliefs and literature, and we often forget that two-thirds of humanity believe in reincarnation. In the West the major religions do not teach this law; indeed, they often oppose it. Furthermore, in a recent public opinion poll in France, it was found that, regardless of the religious affiliation, 20% of French people (one out of five) believe in reincarnation. In most mystical movements this belief is not a dogma, but a proposal for reflection. If you admit the logic of it intellectually, and believe in it sincerely, you cannot fail to see its practical applications working everywhere and in all circumstances. Otherwise, this belief would not be a conviction, and it would be useless to you in conducting your life. The dangerous ego would re-assert its supremacy and its unhealthy, partial judgements. Knowing the Rosicrucians and the strength of their convictions, I am convinced that those among them who, like me, believe solidly in reincarnation were not at all surprised to witness Christian Bernard's rapid rise through the ranks of our Order to the great mastery he has just reached. They agree with me that for the continuity of the Order in the cosmically foreseen circumstances of our age and traditions, a soul-personality was born in an appropriate family and milieu in order to fulfill, at a fixed time, the mission that falls to him in this existence. It is evident that service on the highest plane of our Order necessitates a long education and the acquisition of an interior state comprised of obedience, acceptance, and receptivity, where doubt can at no time occur. Under these conditions, where other than in a home already dedicated to the same service could such a soul-personality and its mental medium be more efficiently formed? Nothing that this service implies would be new or repulsive to a person who has grown up among those already performing this service.

In other words, the first training is received in an appropriate environment. In this way, conviction, solidity of principles, unshakable certainty, and knowledge all the more necessary in all fields will be acquired. One of these fields is the practical domain in which our Order gets its teachings. There are two major aspects of Rosicrucian teachings. One is scientific and of this world. It must be learned in all its details. The other has to do with multiple, difficult, and often changeable elements that require careful management and very long apprenticeship.

But all of this, in spite of its essential nature, is basic only to those who believe in reincarnation, and that is not the case with all the Rosicrucians. I must recognize the fact, however, that, in regard to Christian Bernard I came to these conclusions after the fact. I certainly have felt since he was a child that he would one day be drawn to mysticism, and I tried to answer his questions when I was with him, but I didn't know which mystical path he would take. On that subject, I would have insisted without reserve that he make his own free choice. It was when he was twelve years old that I understood, with unspeakable joy, that his choice would be the Rosy Cross, and thus our Order. Then later he sent a letter that I suggested he write to our Imperator, who asked me to authorize Christian to attend all the convocations or conventions where I would be present. That was the 6th of May, 1966. The first convocation he attended was held at the Jeanne Guesdon Paris Chapter, and strangely enough, the Master who received him was the same person who served this function at the installation of the new Grand Master: Maurice Bellofiore. When he was fourteen, Christian was invited to spend a month with our Imperator in San Jose and to help out at Rosicrucian Park. When I met our Imperator and his wife Gladys later, they both told me simply "For Christian, a yes is a yes, and a no is a no."

At the age of fifteen, on his birthday, he affirmed his choice of our Order, by asking the Imperator, at my suggestion, to allow fifteen-year-olds, with their parent's consent, to join the A.M.O.R.C. This had never been done before. He got what he asked for, and this was to become the general rule in French-speaking countries.

He was then a Rosicrucian, but that did not mean that he was bound to serve our Order some day. I was very happy that he chose my mystical path. However, did I want him to join in active service at the Grand Lodge? Frankly, I can't say so. He was pursuing normal studies, and my wife and I foresaw several careers that he might have liked. My wife, especially, had a thousand plans for him. Mystical service is rigorous and difficult. At a certain level, it implies and requires that family life come last, because of the singular work you are trying to achieve. I hardly saw my son when he was growing up. He was twelve, then fifteen, then older. Having to travel a lot in the service of our Order, I saw him and my wife only periodically. My wife was often alone, and alone she had to take care of him. She did it with love and selflessness that only a mother can give, with admirable devotion that was admired by our neighbors and friends. But I decided to send him to boarding school when he was eleven. Service must come first, even before my devoted wife's wishes or those of my son who had come to terms with being on his own, while facing solitude, along with solidarity and fraternity among other young people of his own age. He was our only son, and it was necessary to avoid his having to be restricted because of this fact. Perhaps you are familiar with some of the human aspects of mystical service. Perhaps you, my dear friends, can answer better than I the question of whether as a father I would want my son to guarantee the continuity of service. Or whether his mother, thinking of his future wife and the possible grandchildren, would wish upon them the sorts of sacrifice that she and Christian had to make, to see him follow in my footsteps, keeping in mind the consequences of this eventuality, their effect on family life and other dangers that few Rosicrucians doubt and I can't talk about.

But these purely human and physical considerations simply and naturally vanish before the cosmic entirety that we are immersed in when faced with the laws of spiritual evolution, tradition, and initiation. These were merely our natural, physical reactions. We repressed them quickly. And when he was eighteen, having chosen an education that would prepare him to enter into Rosicrucian service with few delays, if he should so choose, he was given the choice of a career. His enthusiastic acceptance made us give up all the other plans and hopes we had had for his future. Christian Bernard made a free choice. I welcomed him aboard. That is when I saw the light and understood the principles of the doctrine of reincarnation and how they applied to this personal situation. I gave thanks to the cosmic majesty and will. An infinite peace came into my being. My wife was filled with joy. Another proof, if we needed one, of the cosmic intentions and of what He had decreed, had appeared inescapably at the very moment He had decided upon.

Christian Bernard started a hard apprenticeship. He was shaped according to the needs of the Grand Lodge and its members, in a very ordinary way from outsiders' point of view. When his education was more or less complete, a few years later, he was married and had children. Then I asked the Supreme Council and the Office to act. So he became the Grand Master in the first months of 1975. My duties then as Supreme Legate, as a matter of fact, were becoming more and more demanding. These incessant demands on my time and attention justified my delegating authority to Christian, although it was an unprecedented move at that time. And that is how a number of you have gotten to know him since he took the office of Grand Secretary. Under my supervision, he has presided over all the Rosicrucian conclaves, congresses, and assemblies, presenting messages and conducting mystical experiments. He has travelled everywhere in our vast jurisdiction visiting numerous affiliated organizations.

He has reorganized certain territories, named new grand counsellors and regional monitors, authorized new affiliates, adding as many as I myself had added. He has expanded public discussions, and working with me, he has taken care of the expansion of our Order. Even at the Grand Lodge he has suggested and developed, with my wholehearted support, several kinds of modernization in order to improve the service for our members.

It was in San Jose on the 18th of March, 1977, that I saw Christian Bernard invested with the responsibilities of the office of Grand Master and ritually installed by our Imperator himself. The Supreme Council, at my request, voted for him unanimously. I was in San Jose to attend the annual meeting of the Supreme Bureau. At that time they ratified Christian's election. I must admit that I voted affirmatively at that great moment when it was obvious that it was going to be unanimous. It was necessary to hold an election, and by my yes vote I put an end, ipso facto, to my responsibilities as Grand Master that I had assumed up to that time. It put the stamp of approval on a situation and set of practices that I had already set in motion. Besides, the unanimity of those representative and competent people encouraged Christian to engage in the great mission that was imparted to him. Knowing this, I can say that his first reaction, even though he was fully aware of the fact that to serve is a privilege, was to think that things were better off left as they had been. That is what he told me modestly when he got the official notice from our Imperator. We talked at length about his duties, and about the physical impossibility of my continuing to do two jobs at once. As I had thought, the unanimous vote had made a very strong impression on him, and when he referred to his young age, I reminded him that our Imperator at the age of twenty had assumed the second highest function of the Order, that of Supreme Secretary. And if Christian had been judged capable, it was an expression of cosmic will. I understood what was going on in his mind, as it has for others, for I had gone through the same experience myself. I counselled him to meditate at length, and to give his answer with all interior certainty. Forty-eight hours later, he accepted with, in his own words, "humility and acceptance the opportunity to give further service." He definitely made his own choice.

The official installation of Christian Bernard as Grand Master of our Order in French-speaking countries began at seven-thirty on the morning of Sunday the 7th of August, 1977, in the presence of four thousand Rosicrucians who filled the auditorium. The night before I had solemnly given up my prerogatives as Grand Master, and so I took my place in the ceremony as Supreme Legate among the Grand Masters who were present. I can't describe that secret ceremony to you in writing, but I can tell you that it was very moving.

When the new Grand Master was led in by the Guardian, wearing a simple white robe without any decoration, I felt a very deep emotion. So it was that the torch was passed on! To my son! He was taking on a heavy load; to try out the ways of serving, to share the suffering of others, to undergo exceptional mystic experiences, but also to suffer the incomprehension that some people would show, a suffering largely made up for by the love and support shown by many others. He would go his way, sustained by invisible and powerful presences, forgetting himself, thinking only of serving and obeying, even if he should be humanly misunderstood. Then slowly my emotions subsided, and I followed the new Grand Master on his path. I listened to him take his solemn oath to defend our Order, even to the death, to serve. I thought I wouldn't feel anything particular at that point. However, at the moment when our Imperator effected the initiatic transmission and said "Christian Bernard, I invest in you the authority and power of the Grand Master," being perfectly conscious, I had the feeling that something was leaving me at the level of the solar plexus, and entering Christian at the very moment when our Imperator placed the magisterial stole on his shoulders. The feeling was so distinct, so physical, that at first I thought that the little cross that I always wear on my breast had fallen off, and I checked it quickly with my hand. The cross was where it was supposed to be, and I had once again just experienced the mystical scope of every ceremony or ritual gesture. Whatever is below is as whatever is above, and whatever takes place in time and space in the bosom of a mystical Order is the manifestation of a superior power. In reality, all we do is carry out the omniscient will that brings about in the invisible world whatever the gesture symbolizes in the visible world.

You know, my dear friends, that I rarely share my interior mystical experiences, or others that I may have. In this regard, Christian is like me because, except for when I have to give him some advice on one matter or another, he behaves in exactly the same way. To refer to one's own experiences is doubtless intellectually and emotionally interesting to others, but to do so is to make others forget the true meaning of their own mystical path, and it can sometimes discourage them. The first duty of a mystic is to learn how to be silent. Nevertheless, I didn't hesitate to tell you about what happened during the installation of your new Grand Master. It seemed useful and important to tell you and so I did.

What else can I tell you about Christian Bernard? A lot of you are familiar with him already and others of you are going to get to know him better. But since, for the first and last time, I value my duty to hold forth about him as a person, I will share a few friendly observations of my own. Naturally, in the triangle that makes up all beings, even the wisest, the most evolved, and those who are taking upon themselves the burdens of great work, one of the points, the one that makes us become incarnated so that we have to express ourselves through a physical and mental medium, is necessarily limiting and restrictive. It is our objective personality with all its tendencies and characteristics, etc. But we forget too often that the choice the Cosmic makes to accomplish a mission takes this objective aspect into account and includes it in the nature and scope of a mission. Another way to say this is that whatever we, within the narrow limitations of our human understanding, might see as an imperfection or even a fault, and so criticize it, the Cosmic Himself in His infinite wisdom, and in His omniscience, considers it as a necessary element in the complete realization of the mission to be accomplished. All the Oriental mystics have known for thousands of years and emphasize it in their conception of the guru or teacher. In the West we forget this important aspect, and that's too bad because it doesn't only apply to those who have a particular mission or a great quest to fulfill, but also to all human beings, at whatever level of evolution they have achieved. In regard to this matter, it is easy to see that Christian, like all of us, has his objective personality and character. These were chosen for the job he has to do, just as our own were chosen for whatever we are to do or become. The Cosmic is everything, and we are, all of us, an integral part of the Cosmic.

It is surely easier to speak about what we call qualities among other people, and as mystics that is what we have to strive to do constantly. I observed that for Christian the predominating quality was his straightforwardness. "His yes is a yes and his no is a no," was the opinion of Ralph M. Lewis and his wife. He is no different now. Another of his qualities that his Rosicrucian friends have told me about is his humility. He bravely faces all challenges, gives directions, counsels, and gives instructions that seem appropriate to him. But he insists on remaining behind the scenes. He feels the needs of other people, he quickly perceives their abilities, and he knows how to use these capabilities in bringing about their successes. He is happy in the joy of others, and if he was the cause of success, he never steps forward to claim any attention. Furthermore, he listens confidently and with attention to others before deciding how to deal with their problems in accordance with the scrupulous loyalty that he maintains in relation to our Order, its traditions and established rules. Even though he has the last word in taking his final decisions, he is a firm believer in the process that takes the words of everyone involved into account—collegiality—before the final responsibilities are assigned. He knows that the burden of our immediate direction and perpetuation falls on him, but he also knows that our Order is a community and especially a big family where everyone knows his place and where everyone can and must work with him. His mysticism is very deep while remaining discrete. His goodwill and his love for others are limitless, however hidden they may be beneath an apparent reserve that at first glance may be taken wrongly as coldness. He has an extreme sensibility without being at all vulnerable. Criticism doesn't seem to bother him, even though he knows how to learn from it. He is highly respectful of the private lives of others and he values the courtesy that he himself constantly strives to show. Courteous firmness that he holds to in all circumstances seems preferable to him than aggressivity, except in extreme and exceptional circumstances. He always disapproves of vulgarity. He values humor and wholesome jokes. For him, both are necessary relaxation. He knows how to be quiet and watch silently, preferring, in order to manage better, to think and meditate rather than talk or argue uselessly, with the result that what he is thinking remains indecipherable before he expresses it. His love for others, moreover, makes him communicate greatly as soon as an intimacy is established, and he is always there. His personality is deeply engaging to those who know him and are aware of him beyond the exterior.

But he remains convinced—and this is perhaps the most important—that he is fulfilling a mission of service, and consequently, that he is first and foremost a servant, and, in any case, he has a large capacity for work.

I could naturally go on at great length about your Grand Master, but I think that the most essential has been said. I am perfectly aware that he would not approve and would be embarrassed to know that I have spent so much time talking about him in this letter, and doubtless he would be astonished by the fact that I thought it necessary to do so. He would also be astonished to learn that his human and psychological nature was so familiar to me, since I have never given him reason to think that I would observe and analyze him, who observes and analyzes so many others without their suspecting it. After having reflected and meditated about this at great length, I came to the firm conclusion that it was my duty to tell you about Christian Bernard in this *Letter from Nowhere,* as I have done. Those of you who have known me for many years will see that I have approached this topic completely impartially and impersonally, without taking our blood-ties into account. Or maybe I did! Without them, I would certainly have been more laudatory toward him. You can expect me to be just as objective in regard to others who will follow Christian. It is this conviction that brought me to the conclusion that you wanted me to analyze the man elected to my former position. I believe then that I have responded to your quiet appeal, and I will conclude in affirming with all my heart, my dear friends, that we have a very good Grand Master at the head of our organization, and we should rejoice in this fact. I hope that no malicious or restrictive influences manifest themselves around him in the future, but I know that in him and his work, no matter what the situation, through the love of peace, he will live his whole life as an exceptional person, efficient, competent, and a Grand Master.

An interesting question that you might ask is the following: "What is the cosmic reason for all these changes that we have witnessed and that marked the culminating point of the worldwide Convention in Paris?" This question is all the more judicious, for in addition to the Grand Master of our jurisdiction, another, that of the Nordic Grand Lodge, a new entity that combines several very old Grand Lodges, was installed. The Grand Master of the English and Spanish-speaking countries was changed at the same time. This new Grand Master is Robert Daniels. Other important interior changes also took place. Things went even further to involve others outside our Order. A young man of twenty-five years recently became the Master of the most powerful Sufi community in the world. The elders, like our Supreme Council, elected him to succeed his deceased father. He paid me a courteous and affectionate visit a few months ago. In the exiled Tibetan community, the Rimpoches (the Precious or the Venerables), particularly those who visit the West, are for the most part between twenty-three and twenty-seven years of age, and I know of an aged Rimpoche living in Normandy who is preparing his son to succeed him.

No precise answer can be given to the question asked. It is easy to see that such changes are cosmically ordained and brought about. It seems as if the pieces are put in place by the Cosmic, and mankind is beginning a new stage of development. Since so many young people have been called to do great service, it must be for a double reason. On the one hand, these young people have been less influenced, or not influenced at all, by the preceding cycle. They are, so to speak, new and exempt from all the influences, beliefs and mental habits of the past that were dogmatic and restrictive, and so on. They are thus, in all their being, freer and more available to be transmitters of the cosmic will and wisdom and tools for the Cosmic to use in this new stage of development. On the other hand, it could be that for whatever is being prepared and coming about, the Cosmic needs servants who, because of their youth, have the possibility of lasting a lot longer in carrying out their sustained tasks. We could add that for the long stage of development that is beginning, the dynamism and enthusiasm of youth are essential. This is all we can logically understand and admit at this point. Cosmic plans are set, and they will unfold and become apparent slowly and progressively. I believe that these plans will unfold and reveal themselves precisely through the mission and acts of these great servants who have just become or already are enthroned in their heavy responsibilities. In the realm of tradition and initiation there are no coincidences. The world-wide Convention of our Order, consequently, took place at a definite moment of human evolution. So we see its importance and understand that it had to be such an event.

The fact that young people, for the reasons just cited, are assuming responsibilities on the highest plane should not in any manner suggest that the old will be neglected or forgotten in the new order of things. First, and this is important, it was precisely the old who chose and elected them. Taking that into account, I don't think that any of these young leaders has ever had, not even for a moment, the idea of setting up an age distinction among those they are in charge of from now on. I could even affirm that they are guided by feelings completely different from those we might too hastily ascribe to them. The best proof of this was brought to me while I was writing this *Letter from Nowhere*. Grand Master Christian Bernard sent me a circular that was distributed to those in charge of local and territorial jurisdictions of French-speaking countries. It contained these lines addressed to those we call the Old Venerables in our Order. I'm convinced that it expresses sentiments identical to those that young people in charge elsewhere in authentic traditions would approve of. I quote this excerpt that is clear and telling to me:

> "Time, moreover, goes fast, and youth becomes a memory very quickly. It is the same for me, and the day will quickly come when our first contacts together will reside only in our memories. Also it is important for me to repeat today something I have often said. In our Order there is not, and there never will be, younger and older members. I will never think about any frater or soror according to their age. Every Rosicrucian has a perpetual youth that is in his heart and in his mystical hope. It is simply that certain people are more advanced than others on the path of light. Their life experience and their mystical experience will always be for everybody, and especially for me, a precious gift that will be of great benefit to us if they will freely share it with us. So I hereby salute our Old Venerables. They are an example to me, and I will always appreciate the good advice that they graciously give me.

May they feel constantly surrounded by those who, like me, are full of ardor and enthusiasm in the service of our Rosy Cross and in the service of those who still err in the forest of error..."

My dear friends, once again a *Letter from Nowhere* has brought us together, you and I, and today we have looked at some important questions that are very close to our mystical preoccupation, of which the future will perhaps reveal again their scope. In each *Letter from Nowhere* I will go on expressing everything it seems necessary to me in order to communicate, comment on, and share with you without constraint.

As I said at the beginning, I'll soon be going on a long trip. On my return I'll transmit to you what I have received and what I'm permitted to tell you. So the subject of my next letter is here and now already anticipated.

Until we are together again, I send each one of you, dear friends, my fraternal thoughts, and I remind you of the gratitude I feel for the support you give to the *Letter from Nowhere*.

                              Very sincerely yours,
                              Raymond Bernard

4

DECEMBER 1977

The Spirit of India

Dear Friends,

Let's forget the Western world today, and wake up in a different universe, a world of elsewhere, in a word, India. That's what we call it now, even though its diversity and innumerable aspects justify the older name. But India or the Indies, what does it matter? It is only the same continent, the same earth, the same experience.

Contrary to what people generally believe, in spite of its tropical and often hot climate, India lies entirely in the Northern Hemisphere. This fact did not prevent the heat from being unbearable at the end of September, 1977. The monsoon in 1977 was disastrous, and the heat, usually bearable, was overwhelming, and the friend who accompanied me suffered from it. Being different from me, he puts up better with the cold and regions like the Himalayas, regions where I am barely comfortable. Because of India's immense size, every guide compares the length of its coastline (5,600 kilometers) to the distance between New York and Paris! It is the seventh largest country in the world. The length of its frontiers, 16,000 kilometers, is longer than the diameter of the earth. There are monotonous plains, but basically no more monotonous than others because of the extreme diversity of nature, covering most of the country. I think I may be wrong to apply the term monotonous to the Indo-Gangetic plain that extends over 300 kilometers, forming the basins of three sacred rivers that we will look at together. The Indus, the Ganges, and the Brahmaputra fertilize this marvelous plain, but what explains the identical climate everywhere is evidently the fact that from Delhi to the Bay of Bengal, a distance of more than 1500 kilometers, the difference in altitude is only 200 meters! The country extends to the south across the Tropic of Cancer and ends in a peninsula that bathes on the east in the Gulf of Bengal, and on the west in the Sea of Oman or the Arabian Sea, and off the point of the peninsula the Straits of Palk separate India from the island of Ceylon, now known as Sri Lanka. There you have the Indian plain succinctly described. The peninsula is cut by the mountain chains Vindhya and Aralavi that form escarpments called ghats, and with the ocean all around, these are flat plains of sometimes luxuriant vegetation. But India is not only that, because there are the Himalayas, whose imposing, impressive, mystical chain separates India and China. Between them lies Nepal, with Sikkim, where we are going, on the east, and Bhutan, which we will not visit this time. The Himalayas, with all those summits, is really the roof of the world. We will go there and collect facts, experiences, and knowledge that you will appreciate.

Such is the general setting of our adventure, of our pilgrimage to ancient sources—a setting extending beyond the world, a prestigious setting, a unique scene of a thousand lights. Our entry was made at the beginning of the so-called cool season. This extends from October to the end of February, followed at the beginning of April to the beginning of June by the warm season. Then the rainy season begins, which is supposed to stop at the end of September, but which, this year, is lasting much longer.

I mentioned the monsoon and I'll add a few words on that subject. It is a very impressive natural occurrence of which we in the West have a quite inexact idea. None of our storms is really comparable to it. In India the monsoon comes abruptly, and in a few minutes all communication is cut off and towns and fields are inundated. The rivers go over their banks for hundreds of meters and mud covers everything, creating fertility, that's true, but also causing cruel destruction. This is what happened in 1977, and as late as the end of October, I saw vast regions still flooded. Man is powerless against unchained elements in the rhythm of the seasons. I can't help thinking, however, of our happy vacation time, from June to September in France, when we laugh and relax here; over there they run away, and weep, and wait. How often in the middle of a certainly necessary and deserved rest have we sent thoughts and prayers toward the traditional and accepted unhappiness of a whole people? But there is so much misery in that exceptional and holy land that the monsoon is only the most spectacular one, as we will establish later on.

To complete this overview and in order to understand what I'll explain later, a few words about the population of India and about their languages will be useful. India has almost 550 million people, of whom about 100 million live in large and small towns, but migration toward the towns is increasing on the part of the people looking for the work and education they can find there. To look forward to the future, we can foresee that in thirty-five years the population of the towns in India will increase by 100%. Obviously, that is a disturbing, even frightening phenomenon. This population is made up of differing races. The oldest race, which came to India between the Old Stone Age and the historical age, are the Dravidians. This dark-colored race, up until the 15th Century, was pushed toward the east and south by waves of invaders coming from Central Asia, the Indo-Europeans. They remain one of the predominant racial elements in India. Even today a great number of primitive tribes live in the country's vast forests. In the mountainous valleys of the north-west, there live the only blond people, mixed with Mediterranean and eastern Semitic types.

There are a lot of other racial types, notably the Mongoloid people who have mixed with other groups and live in the valleys near the mountains to the north and west. As for languages, fourteen main languages and 250 dialects are recognized! The most common is Hindi, spoken by half of the people. It is spoken by most of the people in Northern India. The main languages of that part of the country, Punjabi, Gujarati, Orya, and Bengali, comprise the basic elements of Hindustani. On the other hand, except for the words derived from the sacred language of the ancient Hindus, Sanskrit, the languages spoken in Southern India are remarkably different from Hindi. These languages are called Dravidian, and for the record I'll name some of them: Telugu, Kannada, Malayalam, and Tamil.

But the language that permits India to survive as a national entity, the one without which no unity would be possible, is English, and they will tell you everywhere that if it were not for the long British presence in India, this would not be the case today. The British presence is fully justified by this fact. Without English, India would not be a country today. In any case, it is striking to observe that modern India does not reject the period of English colonization. They have purely and simply integrated it into their history, and no monuments from the British era, even those representing important personages of the colonization, have been destroyed. Everything remains as it was, and the guides, in pointing them out, refer respectfully to the old days, showing the intelligence of a people that denies nothing, and in whom pride and a sense of the practical have combined. They refuse to suppress an indelible page of their history. Today's Indian handwriting originated in the brahmi. This kind of writing, the Devanagari, disappeared in the fourth century before Jesus Christ. Indian writing is very angular, but it becomes less so as you go southward.

To conclude this presentation, I will point out that India is made up of 19 states in 10 territories, the whole forming a political entity called the Indian Union. If you are interested, you can find out all about these regions on any detailed map of the country. It is to be understood that in telling you about certain meetings and specifying the places where they took place, I will give you all the necessary geographical information.

In giving you this preliminary information, I am certainly aware that these matters may bore certain readers, but how else can you approach these special subjects without having, before all, put them in their own special contexts? Many books have been written about India that tell about experiences or teach precious lessons with no mention of the context. The results of these books has often been incomprehensibility, even in our time. Many writers have imagined that all they had to do was to go to India and meet the Masters and get wisdom and initiation. They forgot that India is a big place where very different people live in diverse conditions in a difficult climate. They don't take these matters into account. They forget that the natives, whose problems are immense, disconcerting, and even tormenting, must live with misery, unhappiness, sickness, and often famine. In brief, this country of such rich traditions and rare knowledge is in development, a kind expression that hides their horror. It is one country in the world today where, perhaps, it is harder than ever to find wisdom, because you have to get beyond the externals and follow a line of inquiry that gets below appearances, unless as in my case, others with a special mission show you the way. I have seen a lot of unhappiness in the world, and I have seen the sad daily lives of people who have nothing. However, I had never seen the sort of abject poverty that I saw in India. It would take pages and pages to describe, yet incompletely, the suffering and unhappiness of millions of men and women.

Up to this point I have described the geographical and linguistic aspects of India. You know the basic facts about this matter, without which India would be only a word full of mirages and abstractions. You have got to think about the positive side of a country full of rich potentialities, in spite of an endemic sadness. Here I will devote a few more lines to this depressing but real subject. You may come back at me with the observation that India has made real progress, that India has the atomic bomb (is this progress?), that a lot of development is going on. But I persist in pointing out that taking a few steps forward in a world where misery reigns can't be compared to what is happening elsewhere in the secure Western world, where great leaps forward have been accomplished, making India seem to be going backwards. Take a simple example: in the rich countries, we have to go on diets to compensate for our over-eating in our consumer societies where we have too much of everything. In India, no diet could be invented that would make up for poverty. In India, many people go hungry, many people don't have a roof over their heads, many people are sick with diseases already conquered or forgotten elsewhere—tuberculosis, leprosy, and many others. I asked this question, and so did my companion: do the numerous tourists in their opulent hotels, far away from the people, and during their fascinating visits to the monuments of the past, in their haste to see as much as possible in twenty days, or fifteen days, or even in eight (!), ever realize the extent of the tragedy they are wallowing in? I doubt it, and that is perhaps more tragic than the tragedy itself.

As for me, every day I suffered, and every day I wept. My companion, who tried at first to ignore the feelings of compassion, was moved very deeply in his heart. Like me, he saw and he knew... There is no place in India, whether in the cities, the villages, or the countryside, where people are not begging. When you get out of an automobile, you are surrounded by children, their hands raised toward you, repeating the Persian and Arabic word that has practically become international and is used in all poor countries: *baksheesh, baksheesh*. If, moved by pity, or just wanting to be left alone, you weakly give in, you quickly regret your error, because the one you have given money too tells the others out loud or by means of some sign, and then you are followed by a crowd of children who become more and more aggressive.

In order to resist you've got to remember that over there begging is a profession, a lucrative profession, and there are a lot of serious charitable organizations in India that could make much better use of the money you are giving away. They say that the authorities are trying to uproot this evil. It should be noted, however, that the Indians give alms for religious reasons. The beggars near the temples do a real service for the pilgrims who believe they gain merit in giving alms to the poor. And how, in spite of these warnings, can you keep from giving in from time to time, when your whole being is roused with compassion? I'll give you just two examples.

At Varanasi, the real name of Benares, we visited the monkey temple under the watchful eye of a guide who protected us from the monkeys' attack. They like to bite. He used a stick to keep them away, or to some he gave food bought at the entrance. Going in, I at first noticed something in the darkness that appeared to be creeping, and the thing quickly drew close to us. It was a little boy about ten years old, half naked. He was crawling on all fours, his spine horribly twisted, his pale smiling face raised toward us. He said nothing. Yet, there was no way to misunderstand. Didn't he, much more than any others, deserve alms? But we didn't give in at the moment, and our visit proceeded normally. Leaving the temple and arriving at our car, I felt a presence behind us. It was the little boy! He looked at us silently with his sweet eyes. I couldn't resist any longer. Getting into the car to protect myself from the others, I handed him a rupee through the window, and quickly rolled it up. Perhaps he was grateful simply for the sympathy that had been extended to him, because my gesture was full of love. He stayed there until we left. When the car started, his smile grew larger and he raised his hand and blew us a kiss that overwhelmed our being.

We were in Allahabad for some mystical purposes that I'll tell you about when the time comes in this letter to write about the transcendental aspects of my trip. It was the afternoon of our first day in that holy city. We had visited the underground temples and were going away from the sacred river. The next day there was to be a pilgrimage, so a large number of beggars could be expected all along the road, but today there were only a few there. We tried to ignore them, and we were in the car, ready to leave. I was suddenly attracted by pleading eyes. There was a leper with incredible sores, whose forearms as well as his face were eaten away by the disease. "Wait a minute," I said to the driver. I ran over to the leper, dropped my alms into the bowl in front of him. My inner state was indescribable. I quickly touched his head and his poor face. Then I ran away, ashamed of such misfortune, and once in the car, I discreetly let my tears flow. My God! So much misery, so much misery!

The next day, in the same place, the lepers were innumerable. We went among them, staring straight ahead, and it was a tortured groan and cries of anguish that, in spite of ourselves, got our attention. A woman stood there, a mass of bloody flesh. A leper in the last stages of her illness. A leper dying among lepers. We kept on going, in a despondency that turned us in upon ourselves in intense compassion, and at this concentrated moment of pain, having walked far past the car, it caught up with us. I told our guide what I had felt, and he, although deeply religious—I'll speak about him later on—answered to our astonishment: "I don't feel any pity for them! Here in India there are many leprosariums where they could be taken care of or even cured! They don't want to. They would rather beg, every day, here!" Perhaps, but they are at home in the world, and if they refuse to be separated, isn't it surely to imagine themselves alive with the living, in order not to add an intolerable moral suffering to the pain in their bodies? And also, as we will see, the religion in this country is the very foundation of existence and behavior. Everyone knows, believes in, and lives the law of karma, and everyone, in his thoughts, connects his life to his understanding of reincarnation. It is thus impossible to judge in this matter, and I refuse to do so any more than I would elsewhere. Nevertheless, I'll express an opinion later, but it will be based on everything taken together and not on peculiar customs or the behavior of castes or groups.

Economically and socially India is in a nearly tragic condition, and I can't do much more, in this letter or the one to follow, than to write about the caste system, which, even though it is officially suppressed, in reality remains in place. You will certainly be surprised to learn that I approve of this system, certainly not in the excesses that have characterized it over the centuries, but in the original concept. In India there are a few people who have amassed colossal fortunes, a number less privileged who, in different professions, have enough income to allow them to live in a satisfactory fashion, and then there are the masses, some of whom have to make do with miserable salaries and subsistence. Below them are those who have to survive with nothing coming in, or nearly nothing. In the countryside, the peasants, in their miserable houses of wattle and daub, of wood or bamboo, raise whatever they must in order to survive, and try, even in depriving themselves, to sell, for a few rupees, a hypothetical surplus in order to buy basic necessities.

I will not pursue this subject. It would take pages and pages to look into it, even superficially. I will simply say that in India, misery assails you constantly and everywhere. For example, to give you a partial idea of the standard of living, one rupee, that is 60 French centimes (around 15 cents American), makes a very good tip, for some even a royal tip, and few people make more than 200 rupees a month, the equivalent of 120 French francs. In fact, an Indian worker makes every year what the average French worker makes in two weeks! Social programs are practically non-existent, but, nevertheless, in India, contrary to what is generally believed to be true, medicine is not in short supply. There is more than is needed. The question is whether people are able to buy it, and there is the problem, I think. Medicine is expensive, and with such salaries—if you have one—how can you get it when you hardly have enough to live on?

You understand, then, that in India there is simply not enough money. Children, adolescents, adults, old people, men and women are obsessed with the gain or loss of a few pennies. The word rupee affects everybody's mind and determines behavior. But it is not just a vain attraction to money that motivates these unhappy people; it is that money is essential, that is, necessary to their survival, in the full sense of that term. This misery is generally hidden, but it is in the cities that it is so obvious that no one can hide it, and even the guides talk about it all the time. In Bombay, and especially in Calcutta, poverty strikes the visitor in the face. As for the Indians, they seem to be used to it. In the center of the cities whole families live on the sidewalks. They are born there, and grow up, and eat their miserable food, and die there. In a corner of the street near our hotel where a mob of people was so thick that no one could walk through it, there were two little girls, five or six years old, sleeping on the ground! That evening we hardly had time to get to our hotel. My friend had unfortunately given some money to a child, and other beggars, women carrying children that they borrowed for this purpose, followed him. So we were often prisoners in our hotels, at least in the big cities. The only way to get out was to hide in our cars and put ourselves under the protection of our guides.

In these circumstances, it is easy to understand the impression we made on other people. Mr. Singh, a Sikh, the most amusing of our guides, one whom I'll write about later, told us what the people at our hotel in Daramsala thought about us. Figuring that our trip must be very expensive—because something reasonably priced is a luxury for those who have nothing—and knowing that we were staying in India for forty-five days, several people supposed, and this was the case elsewhere, that we were two spies looking for information. That explained, afterwards, several unfavorable, even hard, glances and the coldness of several people we talked with. We learned our lesson quickly. As often as possible afterwards we explained the deep reasons behind our stay in India. That helped us to be better understood, and consequently we received efficient cooperation from many people who otherwise might have remained aloof and suspicious.

I can guess some of the questions you want to ask, particularly this one: "So what are the authorities doing about it?" I'll answer that with a few observations, and let you draw your own conclusions. You have certainly heard about Mrs. Indira Gandhi. Up until last year's elections, she was a prime minister who had, or took, considerable power. She had taken exceptional authority into her own hands, declared martial law, and so forth. Many Indians of the poor classes told us confidentially that the mass of people loved her and regarded her as a cult figure for one very simple reason. Mrs. Gandhi actually used her power to serve the people. She reestablished order. She made the airlines take off and land on time (that's no longer the case, far from it!) and she severely punished any shortcomings. Thieves (they are everywhere!) and criminals went into hiding. But above all, she froze the prices and rigorously watched over the economy for the benefit of the people. Her popularity was great, and it still is. However, and this goes without saying, privileged classes were greatly affected by her severity. She was at war every day against the corruption that rages so powerfully in many developing countries. And then election time came. The opposition made demagogic promises. They gave away a lot of money, and they didn't stop at anything to throw that woman out of power. She had become such a mortal danger to them! Mrs. Indira Gandhi lost, and so she stepped down. They had tried to make the public opinion go against her, but unsuccessfully. And the people now groan about their mistakes, but it's too late. Prices went up, laxity spread, and as is always the case, it is the poorest who suffer the most. I report here only that which was given to us confidentially. I don't know how true all this is, but what is true and visible is the misery and its funeral procession of unhappiness and suffering.

Curiously, people in the villages and in the countryside remain attached to their kings, to their local maharajahs, bereft of any political power, nevertheless still venerated, especially by old people. Were these people happier in the old days? I doubt it, but they used to have, in the maharajah of the state, a protector, a counsellor they had access to, and an object of admiration mixed with pride, something that people sometimes powerfully need. What will happen in the future? An aged guide told us: "What this country needs is a Churchill!", meaning a strong man. I wanted to reply, remembering earlier confidences: "But you had Mrs. Indira Gandhi!", but considering the power that she used to have, could she still be powerful enough? We can understand how Marxist ideologies find considerable success in those countries that are so much the prey of poverty and inequality. They won't solve the problems any better. They represent only a possible hope, a lot of promises of a better tomorrow, and that might be an eventual motive or a way of making people be patient. But India doesn't want it. The communist party doesn't attract any attention, and it constantly shatters into factions that oppose each other. It is true that China is very close but, in India, China is a traditional enemy. As for Russia, it belongs to another world, and India has not forgotten the past either in regard to that country.

Finally, and especially, India is an immense territory where the spirit of religion orders everything and determines behavior. Religion suffuses the land and the people. To everyone it is as tangible as the air they breathe, and it is everywhere. We see it. "So," some will say, "Marx was right. India proves that religion is the opiate of the people." That would be a groundless judgement. Formerly, India was rich, very rich and happy, with the same beliefs. She produced prestigious civilizations. But India was broken into several states, and over the ages, unhappiness was brought to it from elsewhere. The religious spirit of India is no way comparable to what it has been known to be in other latitudes. It has nothing to do with social evolution or economic development. India could become rich and prosperous just as it is religiously and keep all the beliefs, because they have nothing to do with political power. These beliefs are so diversified that they could not make up a block of influence, as is done elsewhere for other religions. Religion in India is a personal question. It is in no way a public matter. This is what explains the unrestricted, absolute tolerance that you observe everywhere in that country in regard to religious beliefs.

What India will be tomorrow nobody can foresee. Will she tempt powerful neighbors? I doubt it, but who knows? She will know how to defend herself, in any case. I rather believe that she has immense potentials and an unexploited substratum. We could say, perhaps justly, with all it means in regard to development and power: "when India wakes up!" But India will not menace her neighbors, India will wake up for herself, and she has quite a bit of work to accomplish within her own frontiers. Evidently, this is the business of the Indians themselves. Are they capable, given their temperament? That's the whole problem. A Churchill, a new uplifting ideology? Who can say? The world will soon see, but while we're waiting, we must not be disinterested. We must show solidarity with that land, just as we do with those who suffer and lament in their unhappiness. It's true that India receives aid, and it is little known that India herself gives to her neighbors who need it. The solidarity of poor nations is an example for the better off... They tell me that the situation is slowly improving. I wasn't able to tell, but there is no reason to doubt that better can go along with worse. Let's hope that wealth will rapidly appear, or at least a subsistence for everybody. Moreover, while we are waiting, no one should prevent those, like me, who consider all people brothers and sisters, no matter where they are or where they live, from proclaiming their compassion and weeping before the misery and suffering of a great people.

Before coming to the interesting topic of the religions of India, or telling you about the Tibetans, whom I will give special attention to, before describing fascinating encounters and exceptional experiences, I think it is appropriate to tell you about the caste system, such as it still exists in India, in spite of the constitutional and legal prohibition, and such as it originally was before its degeneration and abuse. This story explains why it is so disapproved of and misunderstood outside of India and within India by a large number of young people, but not by all the young people.

The caste system in India goes back a long, long way, but according to historians, it was established only twenty-five hundred years ago. Degenerating over the course of time, this system came to comprise hundreds of distinct communities, each separated from the others by strict rules regarding diet, professions, and other aspects of existence. It was once thought the castes were set up four thousand years ago (which contradicts the statement of twenty-five hundred years made by certain writers), in order to differentiate between the Aryan invaders and the aboriginal people, so that differences in dress, cults, or physical appearances would be sufficient to mark superior and inferior classes. In fact, the caste system, originally, was based on the application of certain universal laws, such as reincarnation and karma, as they were then understood in the context of the age. The Laws of Manu, moreover, define this system very clearly. There were later tribal fears and other taboos that changed the castes such that they organized according to professions and duties in a very strict mechanism of rigid rules—prohibition of marriage between castes, eating together, etc. The basic castes were and still are the following: the Brahmans, the Kshatriyas, the Vaisyas, the Sudras.

Below these castes were the untouchables who had to do the lowest kinds of work. Mahatma Gandhi tried to rehabilitate the untouchables. He called them Harijans, or children of God.

The Brahmans had rigorous rules regarding the purity of ceremonies. They are the ones who developed the idea of Dharma (duty) that has become the goal of Hindu society. Only the Brahmans were qualified to teach and interpret the holy doctrines. They were, in effect, lay priests. The Kshatriyas were the soldiers, and in time of peace, the administrators. The Vaisyas were the merchants and the artisans. As for the Sudras, they worked in the fields and at humble professions. One writer observed that this system reminded him of Plato's Republic and his categories represented by gold, silver, and bronze. According to Indian understanding, on the other hand, the castes are derived from the god Brahma, and they represent his mouth, arms, legs, and feet. This system was perfectly logical, as it was originally conceived. The Hindus call it *varna-ashrama,* varna signifying color, and ashrama place of refuge, peace and harmony. Its purpose is, consequently, to join together the different categories of human beings harmoniously.

I understand that it would be difficult, from the outside and at first glance, to understand and approve of this system. We are tempted to see the notion of superior and inferior, which is wrong. Each caste, in fact, has its advantages and disadvantages, like every institution. For example, the Brahmans have to refuse the earthly advantages that belong to the Vaisyas, possessions and food, but they benefit exclusively from the life of study and spirituality. It would be difficult for me to go into detail here. A whole book would not be enough. In order to get an excellent understanding of this fascinating subject, especially if you intend to visit India one day, don't forget to read the best and clearest work ever written on this subject and the art of Hindu living, the work that caused me to see India through different eyes: *The Four Senses of Life,* by Alain Danielou. There you will learn about the mode of existence that, in spite of appearances, many Indians continue to observe. Notably, you will learn that once his duty as a man is accomplished, anyone in India can become an outcaste, and be looked upon by all with devotion and respect, in renouncing the world and its works, the only way to knowledge, spirituality and inner enlightenment. Even if you don't intend to go to India, this important book will enlighten you and inspire you to the highest degree.

And this brings me to speak about the Sadhus. They are the Hindu ascetics. There are six million of them! Many of them are real seekers, authentic seekers. They live in the icy hills of the Himalayas or in the deep forests of the South. Also, many of them are only vagabonds. We saw a great number of them on the roads and paths. Most of them live at the expense of pious villagers who are too credulous. A few rare ones among them are perhaps sincere pilgrims, visiting the sanctuaries of India according to ancient traditions. But there are very few Ramdas who are well known for their Pilgrims' Notebooks. Note in passing that there are practically no Sadhus among the Tibetans. We saw one, however, on a road in Sikkim. He had painted a third eye in the middle of his forehead, he wore a hairy animal skin around his loins, and he carried a trident in his hand. They told us that he was mentally unbalanced. It is true that a Tibetan, converted to the cult of Shiva, by definition a Buddhist, is not a typical sight.

In any case, the true Sadhus, the real mystics, begin their quest with a spiritual guide, with a guru. We will have to come back to this point. In the meanwhile, let's remember that a guru is not a tutor, in the Western sense. Certainly, he teaches according to his method, but his presence and his example are at times sufficient to lead the disciple to discover the divine within himself, and it is essential to know that, according to Indian tradition, mystical experience is individual and its basic principles do not permit and have never tempted a real sage to create a school on this basis having only a goal of communicating this experience to others. And so a Western seeker travelling through India is always astonished to find that the gurus or Hindu Masters, who go to Europe and the United States and gain great celebrity and the infatuation of a large following, are throughout India either unknown or looked upon with disdain. It is true, as certain well-informed writers and speakers do not hesitate to declare, that you can be taken aback when you learn of the extreme misery in India and the human and moral problems that exist there. And certain people, calling themselves agents of benevolent groups, go to that country to bring, they say, knowledge, happiness, and even Western health care, when there is so much to do there to improve the lot of millions of wretches. I am not going to go so far as to say , as many never hesitate to do, that the attraction of big money, compared to the weak rupee, is a sufficient motive to explain the arrival of so many visitors calling themselves gurus. Without a doubt, the credulity of a great number of people and the attractiveness to so many of anything that comes from the Orient, have for a long time been the basic reasons for the success of certain of these visitors. But the ease of communication, travel, rapidly accessible information, and even much greater prudence, born of shattered hopes and proven fraudulence, have led the West to be more cautious.

Certainly, authentic gurus or masters have come to our countries and will continue to do so—I'm thinking in particular of the true representatives of Tibetan wisdom, but these people were known and appreciated in their own country. They worked there and consecrated themselves to improving the conditions, perfectly aware of their essential duty to help others. Their visits to the West were and are always discrete. They obstinately avoid all flashy publicity. In a word, they fulfil their mission. The most authentic create no branches or centers. During their visits, at meetings and conferences, they recognize those who have special hope, who can benefit from their wisdom. To them they propose the way of renunciation and sacrifice, that is, they ask them to leave everything behind, to follow them to India, to an ashram that is secret and hard to get to, where the conditions are extremely hard, and where for years they will have to prove that they are ready every day. I visited one of these ashrams. I'll explain how. Then you will understand better why I, perhaps more than others, am always prudent, while remaining naturally tolerant, understanding, well meaning, and cooperative in all things.

Recognized, authentic Masters, Lamas venerated for their lofty science and superior accomplishment, showed their extreme interest in and respect for our traditions. Explicitly, certain ones of them pointed out to us how much they themselves count on us Western seekers, and some of them said that they cannot understand why apprentices of the eternal truths had to seek so far away for what they have at home, on their doorstep. But that is human nature. It has a tendency to appreciate a thing less, even a treasure, if it is too easily accessible! It even has a tendency, unfortunately, to cause the initiate sometimes to see himself as the spectator of the training he receives, to analyze it, even to judge it, in place of simply submitting to it and then, and only then, to measure the effects on himself. So it is that the ego, the great divider, the separator, instead of being mastered, easily remains the master, and interior development is a mirage that he subtly keeps in his power.

It is clear, moreover, that in the sphere of initiation, the principles of direction and transmission are, and remain, intangible. But this direction and transmission must never be tinged with participation, that is, it must never assume a state where the seeker is allowed to express opinions about the techniques or the training received. It is the reverse of what happens in the exterior world where education, not without loss, has come to respond to the demands of those who receive it, and where it is oriented toward preventing rebellion or dissatisfaction. The initiatory technique, on the other hand, maintains and reinforces the notion of authority and firm direction in the interest of the initiates, in such a way that there can never be any alternatives or compromises. This means that on the seeker's part it is precisely a matter of accepting or refusing, and a refusal means a rejection, a rejection that he chooses for himself and for which he is solely responsible. That is what I retain from many important meetings, observations, and conversations with Masters of wisdom. It represents an immense responsibility on the part of the Great Initiatic Orders of our time. I take some comfort in the fact that those unchallenged and revered Oriental Masters were able, with the clairvoyance and certitude that their high accomplishments have given them, to recognize without reservation, and with such assurance the unique value to the West, and even to the whole world, of our traditions. That was, doubtless among others, one of the great lessons of my long trip, a trip that from start to finish was an attentive quest, the results of which, with their direction from On High, far surpassed any of my hopes.

Moreover, before sharing these results with you, I must hold forth at length on the subject of the religions of India, and another letter will have to do with the Tibetans, whose knowledge is extremely interesting. As I said before, my intention in telling you about my trip to India is to allow you to understand that land of light better in all its aspects, even if some of them are limiting or even deceiving. Another way to say this is that I hope that after you have read these letters devoted to this subject, your knowledge of India will have a solid base that will contribute to your later study and reading, so that you can approach the subject with a firm background and the necessary caution. It certainly isn't a question of my giving you an academic course, but more simply to give you a base and some suggestions in my usual way, even if some of my explanations seem to be a little dry.

It is probable that quite a few of you will have read a great deal on this subject and consequently will find here much that you got elsewhere. You will find, however, in these *Letters from Nowhere*, the point of view and the particular experiences that are mine alone. In any case, and I repeat, it would have been unrealistic to tell you about these meetings and unusual experiences without explaining the human and geographical context in which they occurred. Otherwise, the impression you receive would be false and incorrect. Furthermore, I have tried to help you to understand that pearls of wisdom can be found in the worst human and social environments—and that it is necessary to go beyond appearances in order to get at them, in spite of deceiving or even repulsive circumstances. Finally, those among you who may go to India some day will not be paralysed by the exterior appearances of things that you first come across. You won't be shocked or deceived because you will know that in the midst of all there exists a radiant wisdom. I will say even more: these unhappy people teach us a lesson, in spite of their squalor, a lesson about human and religious behavior that we must learn. Please don't talk to me anymore about superstition or idolatry! There is no more superstition or idolatry in India than there is in our Christian West, in our veneration and worship that surround the places of pilgrimage and the statues of the Virgin and the saints. It all depends on understanding, and nobody had better ever judge, especially in regard to that which is sacred.

Let us now look at all the religions of India in broad outline. We can look, first of all, at the statistics in order to gauge their relative influence. These numbers concern the whole population of India, 550 million people:

- 85% are Hindu
- 10% are Muslim
- 2% are Christian
- 1.7% are Sikh
- .06% are Buddhist
- .05% are Jains
- .04% are Zoroastrian

Certain observations are necessary here. The term Hindu refers to an adept of the Hindu religion, not to a native of India. It is an often repeated error to call the inhabitants of the country Hindus. They are Indians. So, every time I refer to a Hindu or Hindus, I am referring to people who are faithful to a religion that is very important in India, and that I will have more to say about. Since the beginning of this letter, when I have wanted to talk about the people of India, I have used the term Indian.

Another observation is necessary. I will have nothing to say about the Christian religion there. We all know about it. It is only necessary to say that the conversion of 2% of the population is relatively recent. In the Indian state of Kerala, on the Malabar coast, you can meet Syrian Christians who claim to have been converted by Saint Thomas. They claim to be the inheritors of the most ancient traditions of the Apostles. The Roman Catholics, in other areas, owe their conversion to a Jesuit who went to India, with the Portuguese in the 16th century, St. Francis Xavier. In the 2% of Christians there are some Protestants. They are there because of British missionaries, and because of a few from Holland.

Let's go back to St. Thomas the Apostle. On the 26th of October, in the last days of our trip, we visited a church in Madras where there is a tomb that is said to be that of St. Thomas. We went to look at it in the sacristy, by a special request, after paying a few rupees. There in a monstrance was a spear point with which the saint had been killed by the king, and a piece of one of St. Thomas' fingers. What surprised me in this encounter with the past was the reaction of my friend. There he was in front of the tomb of this suspect apostle. Would he find there the symbol of all his forgotten doubts? After our long visit and all the wondrous proofs, could he possibly doubt? There is much to think about here.

In regard to the history of the Christians in India, we must keep in mind the cruel persecutions that the Portuguese Catholics wrought upon the people on the west coast in the 16th century, which made the people hate and despise the Westerners. And we must also keep in mind, unfortunately, the fact that Indian Christians, even today, demonstrate a fanaticism and intolerance that brings them unanimous disapproval on the part of other Indians, whose extremely religious temperament has permitted them, over the course of centuries, to assimilate any number of beliefs because of their respect for the sacred and their absolute tolerance. We ran into some Indian Christians. Their arguments and acerbic criticism of their fellow countrymen of other faiths so dismayed us that we asked them if they were really Indians, and they were. According to them, their non-Christian compatriots were lazy and never on time. They didn't like to work, and so on! That 2% would have you believe that the other 98% wasn't worth anything. We were astounded. They wanted our agreement and collusion. Naturally, we didn't consent to that.

On the other hand, the Sikhs, as well as the Jains and the Parsis or followers of Zoroaster, in spite of being few in number are worth greater attention. The same is true of the Buddhists, the percentage of whom, only .06%, may surprise you, since Buddhism was born in India. But Buddhism has become the exclusive religion of most Asian countries, in particular of Tibet. We will spend some time studying it in relation to Tibet.

In the next *Letter from Nowhere* we will turn to this fascinating subject. As in this letter, from time to time I'll mention my trip, but it is later in a forthcoming letter that I will speak at length about the mystical events that largely made it up. You will get a lot more out of it if you devote your attention and interest to the preceding explanations.

So, dear friends, I'll get back to you soon. I want to take this occasion to remind you and your loved ones that I send my best wishes for your success, and I hope that peace comes to the world and that solidarity and fraternity spread among all people wherever they are.

                    Very sincerely yours,
                    Raymond Bernard

5

JANUARY 1978

India's Religious Landscape

Dear Friends,

In the last *Letter from Nowhere* we got acquainted with India. We examined India in regard to its geography and population, and we saw that this immense country, in all its diversity, makes up a continent in itself. Then we looked at the grave problems that India is facing, in particular the appalling misery that permeates it and the whole complement of maladies, and even of famine. We considered a system—the caste system—that could constitute a solution perfectly adapted to the specific needs of those people if it were to return to its original form. I think that I had better go back to this question somewhat later in order for you to understand it better. Then we approached the important subject of religions, and that is the subject we will take up today.

You could say without exaggeration that religion is the very essence of India in all its aspects. Doubtless that is what explains the psychology of those great people, their ways of coping, their ways of life, and what outsiders see, wrongly, as their passivity and apparent acceptance of the unhappy conditions they live under. But India is only partly responsible for those conditions. India isn't a territory separate from the world. It is an integral part, but like so many countries, politely called developing countries, it gets only stingy foreign aid that doesn't correspond to its basic nature and real needs. It is evident that, for all Indians, religion is a great comfort. This would be so even if India were the most developed country on earth. An Indian actually possesses a religious temperament that is the motive of his whole life. This peculiarity can be found elsewhere, of course, for example, in Africa, but India seems to have become—indeed, it is, in reality—the land of light and understanding. It was the repository of millennial truths, and it remains thus. It is the place on earth where the Primordial Tradition was blended, by means of the Rishis or sages, in the earliest times, into differing ways conducive to the diverse aspirations of humankind. But it is also true that if that country were chosen, it is incontestably because, from the beginning, its inhabitants were by temperament the most receptive to that which was destined, by means of them, for humanity, and so they have remained, in spite of invasions and the mixing of races, perhaps partly because of the caste system. It is doubtless also because that land was blessed with a climate and geography that fostered a close link between the Divine and our world, in a way that established an intimate relationship between that which is on high and that which is below. If there are places like these on earth, antennas if you will, India is one of them, as her long spiritual and mystical history proves.

Finally, the people, such as they are and, in the circumstances that surround them, as tragic as they may be, remain by tradition and secular training a perhaps unwitting melting pot, where the essential truths put at humankind's disposal perpetuate themselves in forms multiplied to infinity. This is demonstrated by the fact that even traditions or beliefs born elsewhere have been able to go to India and be welcomed there. In the spiritual domain, India is open to everyone, and this doesn't consist solely of tolerance, but of an inborn disposition in her people, as well as the gift of amalgamation that can welcome and incorporate anything outside itself, while remaining itself. By this infinite possibility of accepting, Hinduism appears to be a religion able to adapt to anything, anytime. It is this religion of such a universal character that we will look into first. We have seen that Hinduism accounts for 85% of the population. What astonishes the foreign visitor in India is the incalculable number of gods, demi-gods and their incarnations in a thousand forms. The Hindus will tell you that they number three million! And immediately the Westerner's reaction leads him to an entirely erroneous conclusion. He talks about idolatry! But all these gods, goddesses, demi-gods, and avatars or incarnations represent only the materialization of cosmic law and a sole God. The Hindus are monotheists. They believe in the unity of the Supreme Being, but they symbolize the powers and the innumerable cosmic and natural processes of God in the universe and the world by agencies, figures, and gods related to natural phenomena. In sum, these innumerable gods are only the diversified phenomena of the unique Noumenon. Many Hindus, certainly a majority, understand it. But over there it is like everywhere else.

In the Christian world, certain social groups not very well developed intellectually, and even less spiritually, join in the cult worship of a saint and a statue, or yet of a Patron Saint of a trade or profession. The same thing naturally exists in India, and some people even have their household gods that are not related to others. On this subject, an Indian Christian, our driver in Benares, who was sectarian and judgmental about his fellow Indians, was satisfied with his religious faith because, he said, he was a simple person who did not understand all those gods. For him, and in this his smirk of disdain was telling, it was all a matter of idols and superstitions. If you look carefully at the facts in their reality, his lack of understanding, which was inculcated in him by rigid and dogmatic teaching, is made obvious in his criticism of his fellow countrymen. He too said they are mostly lazy. Was it not the case that he, himself, had looked for a simple explanation that was intellectually dishonest? For he had not the courage to look beyond appearances in order to contemplate the Unique One, the God of the Indian Sages. But I must not forget that among the 2% of Christians, many of them were recruited from the lowest castes and among the untouchables. Their recruitment elevated them socially to the outcastes, a considerable promotion! Can we see in the bitter criticism of these converts a manifestation of vengeance against their former co-religionists? That would certainly be a very regrettable understanding of their new religious state, and a violation of the essential rule of Christianity: Judge not! Love everyone!

It is in any case shocking to see that, being set in place outside the caste system, only 2% of Indians have opted for Christianity. Our conclusion must be that most people are happy with what they have. If this were not the case, how many Indian people would have welcomed the Christian religion as a way to get them out of their social class? Untouchable to outcaste, a big step. But Hinduism, without changing its essential nature, has been able to integrate Jesus Christ and to consider him as an incarnation of God. There's the difference, and an enormous one it is. I saw in a merchant's shop a print of an engraving of some divine incarnations, and among the Avatars, in the center was Jesus of the Sacred Heart! It didn't surprise me.

In Hinduism, the one Supreme Being materializes a trinity, or a triptych representing the principal powers of God. This trinity is made up of Brahma, Vishnu, and Shiva. One of our guides, a Brahman in Agra, gave us a brilliant explanation, on the 7th of October, of the Hindu trinity, explaining that these three aspects were simply those of a single God. In the last days of our trip we talked to a lot of guides and they were of one mind. They agreed that our function was to pass on this information, that we were a sort of relay for the world outside, and many people would benefit from what we would pass on to them. For example, an aged guide set us down on the steps of an old temple in order to teach us face to face, in Agra, in front of that unforgettable jewel called the Taj Mahal. He spoke to us in English: "In English, Dieu is God. So listen. G means the Generator, the Creator; that is Brahma. O means the Observer, who keeps everything going, the Conserver; that is Vishnu. D means the Destroyer; that is Shiva. And these three gods, this trinity, are all the same. That's God!" Nothing could have been clearer to explain our single God in His fundamental powers—creation, conservation, and destruction.

Brahma was formerly worshipped as being the most important of the trinity, but today very few temples are dedicated to Him and the number of His worshippers is extremely limited. His temples, however, are majestic, like the one in Pushkar (meaning Lotus) that we had the pleasure of visiting after going through some respectful rites at the sacred lake of that city and having put the red spot of devotion on our foreheads. The explanation of this lack of popularity of the cult of Brahma was given to us in a realistic and quite logical fashion by a devout Hindu. "As for Brahma, that's all over. You've got to think about the present and the future. Vishnu the Conserver, and Shiva, the Destroyer, yes, they are always what is current." This declaration on his part was not blasphemy or sacrilege. He knew how to talk about divine powers. If he denied one part, consigning it to an age that has gone past, he was not less respectful of the two others, and by this devotion, of God Himself! Brahma, unlike the two other gods, has no incarnation in his own right. The Sacred Writings of India, the Vedas, put him directly with the Supreme Being. He is represented in statues as having four heads. So Brahma looks out in four directions. These heads are considered to be the incarnation of the four Vedas. Brahma, the first of the Hindu trinity or trimurti, is the god of wisdom. He is thus an important power. Like all the gods, since materialization demands that there be a double polarity, the masculine and the feminine, Brahma has a wife, Saravati. She is the goddess of science. Hindu art shows her, a lute in her hand, mounted on a swan.

The Protector or Conserver of the universe, the second power, Vishnu, is often cited in the Vedas, and he too is an extremely ancient god. His wife, born from sea foam like Venus, is as beautiful as a Greek goddess. They often invoke Lakshmi in India because she rules wealth and prosperity. Vishnu is most often represented as seated or lying on his personal serpent that serves him as a seat or a bed. Of his four hands, in one of the upper ones he holds a seashell that looks like a conch, in the other he holds a disk. In regard to the multiple arms that you find on statues and pictures of the gods, there appears to be a reason for this fact and it is perfectly logical. These arms on the statues and in the pictures allow you to recognize the gods among the figures represented. Naturally, in addition to this logical reason there is another, higher, initiatic reason that is told only to those admitted to share certain secret knowledge, and for this reason, I can't do that, but any advanced seeker ought to be able to figure it out for himself.

If Brahma has no incarnation, Vishnu himself has ten, and among them, the ninth, we find the Buddha, which again demonstrates the extraordinary Hindu faculty of assimilation. But the two main incarnations, the two Avatars that retain the greatest fervor of the faithful, are Rama and Krishna. These incarnations humanize, so to speak, the concept of a more severe god. They put this concept within humankind's reach, and their cult is comparable in the Catholic world to that of the Virgin, for example, or to that of the infant Jesus, whom Krishna resembles in various ways since he is said to be born of an immaculate virgin. The epic poem about Rama is a very long story that is often deeply symbolic. The Ramayana is still recited once a year throughout India over the course of several days, the last of which is a day of great rejoicing, the Dusehra. It corresponds to the last act of the epic when Rama defeats Ravana, the monster with ten heads. The Ramayana is 48,000 verses long, and it must have been written by a single author—Valmiki. Rama naturally has a wife, Sita, who is considered in India as the ideal woman. Rama and Sita are the most loved and popular divinities.

Krishna is the eighth incarnation of Vishnu, and he certainly has become popular even in the West thanks to his devotees wearing saffron-colored robes, their heads shaved, except for a little tuft of hair, accompanying themselves on tambourines, dancing and singing Hare Krishna! (Long live Krishna). The tuft of hair is kept in order to allow Krishna to grab the faithful and pull them up to him at the moment of death. That is obviously a symbol. These devotees are, it must be admitted, attractive. They make a glory of their convictions and that earns respect. On this subject, here is an amusing anecdote. Our visit to Katmandu was over, we had just seen the Living Goddess, and our guide had left us. We were walking toward the main square, when singing and tambourines attracted our attention. Drawing near we witnessed a unique spectacle—American devotees of Krishna on a platform singing and dancing. Hare Krishna! Hare Krishna! My companion and I were the only two foreign spectators. All of the others around the devotees were Nepalese. A very strange spectacle in the heart of Nepal! That was worth a photograph, but my companion had forgotten his camera, but they were still there the next day and the picture was taken.

Rama is, as we have just seen, the central figure of the Ramayana. Krishna is the subject of the Mahabharata, a much longer epic than the Ramayana, since it is composed of 100,000 stanzas. It is in the Mahabharata that we find a work of great wisdom, the Bhagavad Gita, or the Songs of the Very Happy. Krishna, as an infant or a young man, is always represented as a person with a blue body and face. He is always playing a flute. For the Hindus he is the symbol of human, personal love. He is the most lovable and understanding god of all. So he is the one represented in the dances. Most of the sculptures and paintings and Hindu music have to do with him. For girls he is the ideal man, the lover they dream about. When Krishna was a child he was a little devil who played tricks on his mother, but it was his special love affairs with the shepherdesses that have made him so popular. Such a human god as Krishna, a god anyone can understand, explains why so many devotees are absolutely committed to him, and he is, after all, held to be an incarnation of the Supreme Being. In any case, he deserves it.

Shiva is another matter. Outwardly, he seems to be the Destroyer. He is the master of death, of pestilence, of war, and of such disasters as droughts and floods. He doesn't have a home, although he often goes to the Himalayas, to the summit of Mount Kailara to meditate about the punishment inflicted upon him by his divine colleague Brahma, one of whose heads Shiva broke off in a fit of anger. Brahma now forces him to wander through time. Like all the gods, Shiva can be recognized by certain signs. He has belts of twisted serpents around him, or tiger skins around his body, or an eye in the center of his forehead. You also see him holding a cup made up of a human skull, or holding a trident, or sometimes a war axe. Shiva has a famous mount that makes it easy to recognize him in sculptures. That is Nandi, the sacred bull. In southern India Shiva is frequently represented as the cosmic dancer, Nataraja. But in all the temples we visited and elsewhere, Shiva is represented by the lingam or phallus, the emblem of the masculine sexual organ that stands for cosmic energy, the force of creation. Shiva's cult is spectacular. We participated in it on the 24th of September, near Udaipur, in a frequently visited temple. It was at a set time, at five-thirty p.m., that the doors were opened. The faithful rushed in, with us among the last. Like all the faithful, we had bought flowers, and in front of the lingam surrounded by floral garlands, we threw them with a rupee—that's the custom, and there is an explanation, as we'll see later—we placed our hands together in front of our breasts, then in front of our faces, and without speaking ourselves, we were bathed in the vibrations of the word: Shiva! Shiva! that the Shivaites shouted as they passed in front of the lingam, each one alone with himself and the god, in an interior concentration that I have felt so intensely only in India, even in the people in the street, at the moment of prayer. I will come back to this point and to what the temple means to a Hindu. He doesn't spend much time there, just a few moments to salute his god, the real worship being practiced at home, every day, morning and evening, before the family altar, and that goes for the whole Orient, the Tibetans too.

One important point should be made here concerning Shiva. It would be simple to think that the purpose of the faithful's adoration is to appease Shiva by praise, but that would be related to calamities, catastrophes, and maladies that can affect the whole population. This vigorous adoration is similar to what is practiced elsewhere, even among Christians, to ask God for peace, health, or protection. But Shiva is not feared. He is venerated because, as many Hindus told us, he is the god who destroys evil, who destroys that which is detrimental to man and to his evolution or health, that is, to those things that prevent humankind from leaving the cycle of reincarnation. Shiva is, consequently, above all the destroyer of bad actions, bad thoughts, in a word, of evil. This idea is little known. You have never read it in any learned study, and it is worth bringing fully to your attention because Shiva, seen in this way, is a power of the Supreme Being that answers a real need for humankind insofar as he is a creature in evolution.

Of all the goddesses of Hinduism, the most powerful is Parvati, Shiva's wife, who sports different names, according to her powers or attributes. But don't the virgins and the saints, among us Christians, take on qualities relative to whatever attributes you confer on them—Our Lady of the Seven Sadnesses, Saint Julian the Poor, etc.? Parvati, considered a benevolent spirit, is a beautiful woman and attached to her husband. When she is near him she is represented in a loving posture. But she also becomes the queen of battle, with weapons in her hands that will enable her to punish. She is then the terrible Durga. We were in Darjeeling, and in Sikkim at Gangtok, on the 21st and 22nd of October, at the culminating moment of the festivities in honor of the goddess Durga. All the devotees wore colored rice stuck on their foreheads, and they followed the custom for three days. On the evening of the last day, after the joy and the final libations of the day to the goddess, an effigy was burned in the uproar of firecrackers, and that marked the end of the grand puja (ceremony) of Durga. The cries of joy and all the noise of the festivities reminded us of what you see in similar circumstances, in other latitudes, and we heard that last day the racket that presided over the destruction of the goddess Durga, just a short distance from our hotel in Gangtok. Parvati can also appear under the aspect of the goddess who vanquished time, the black and formidable Kali. Her thirsty red tongue hangs from her black face. She wears a collar of skulls. You have to appease her with garlands of flowers. Formerly, barbaric propitiary rites were reserved for her. They are no longer current anywhere for any god, except, strangely and surprisingly, in peaceful Nepal, where once in a while they take place. That was the case on the 14th of October when we were in Katmandu. On that day in honor of Durga every family had bloodily slaughtered an animal.

On the 26th of September, in Jaipur, in the course of a conversation with a couple of Frenchmen, we were advised to be very careful. Tourists were being kidnapped and sacrificed to the goddess Kali. I must say that such news left me skeptical. In spite of the apparently serious manner of the people we were talking to, I took it all as a bad joke of dubious taste. It is true that you can't tell where fanaticism will rear its ugly head, but all the same... During my whole stay in India, and it was a long one, I never noticed the slightest fanatical act or word on anybody's part, and our contacts were such that we were not considered as simple tourists, but as revered visitors, nearly friends. It was a real privilege because contact between Indians and tourists is not encouraged. They show a lot of deference to travellers, but there is little intimacy. But the intimacy we had, or I might say, the complicity, based on our common longing for spiritual truths, was part and parcel of our experience from the beginning to the end of our journey. I had adopted a very simple means. My first words were always "We are not tourists, not ordinary tourists. We are looking for spiritual experiences." To say that human sacrifice could play any part in all of this, something nobody ever mentioned, seemed to me an absurd point and a sort of calumny.

So on the 28th of September, two days later, after having quickly visited Fort Amber, we had the chance to attend a Kali cult meeting. We jumped at the chance and never regretted it. We were the only foreign strangers. There were not many people there, and we were in front of the crowd up against the goddess. A bell behind us kept ringing its strange, captivating sounds. A curious kind of music, a psalmody in two voices was being sung by two priests. My companion and I, surrounded by Hindus, had a remarkable, startling experience. At the end we held out our hands towards the priest who sprinkled holy water on us from a tiny silver pot. We wet our faces with it, and putting several white and red petals on our heads, received the red mark in the middle of our foreheads, once more purifying our hands in the red flame that the priest offered to us. The symbolism was clear as it could be: water, earth (symbolized by flowers), air (the bells) and fire. Each of us left a rupee, and we were led to the door, suffused again by a strange inner experience. But by mistake we were led to the wrong door, one that was tightly sealed, where we were abruptly stopped and directed to the right exit. "Hmm," my companion murmured, "it's not the time to go to forbidden places. Maybe that's the door for sacrifices!" It was a good joke, and we both laughed, as we did so often in the course of our trip. We were getting so much access to strange things that we were constantly having to re-balance ourselves, and good humor—or nearly infantile good humor—helped a great deal.

On the subject of Kali, let's not forget that she is the good and tender Divine Mother that the great Ramakrishna constantly referred to. At the beginning she had been terrible for him, but he had understood, and conquered by his love she became forever his tender mother, his constant preoccupation. However, let's not get ahead of ourselves. I'll come back to Ramakrishna in talking about some ashrams I visited, and I'll do it with devotion, respect, and love. Ramakrishna is a universal Sage, and his accomplishments are examples for us all. Among the important gods I will mention Ganesh, the son of Shiva and Parvati. He is a sympathetic and touching god. He was also the favorite of my companion, and for my part, I liked him very much too. Having his head sliced off by his father in a moment of anger, he had dared to forbid Shiva's entry to Parvati's rooms, on the strict orders of his mother, and she had included her husband in the orders given. At her supplication, Shiva agreed to put the head of the first creature that his guards found on the shoulders of his son. It was the head of a little elephant. So good and faithful Ganesh came back to life with that new head. I tell it like it is. He is attractive and moving. But he is also the god of prudence, prosperity, and especially of wisdom. So you understand why every time we saw a statue, or fresco, or engraving of Ganesh, and that was often, we placed the palms of our hands together in front of our chest, then in front of our faces, to greet him with respect and render sincere homage.

The gods and goddesses that we were just talking about are the most numerous. They are the ones it is necessary to know about. The many others are entirely secondary and do not merit our attention. But if these few remarks have stimulated your further interest, it is sure that you will be tempted to learn more about Hinduism. You should read simple works. I'll suggest two, both available in French: on the one hand, *Living Hinduism,* by Jean Herbert, and on the other, an excellent book to read after you have read the first one, *Hinduism.* The latter is comprised of texts and sacred traditions presented by Anne-Marie Esnoul, with a preface by Oliver Lacombe of the University of Paris. Among the works recommended by the Rosicrucian Editions, you have probably noticed that some of them are about Hindu and Tibetan wisdom. I have read these works myself, and I suggest that you contact Rosicrucian Editions because I'm sure that reading them will be beneficial. So in addition to the two books mentioned above, I have asked that several works be made available: *The Teachings of Ramakrishna, Pilgrim's Notebook,* by Swami Ramdas, and the rather more difficult but inspiring books by Sri Aurobindo, who was lately one of my Teachers, along with works by Satprem, and others. I have just proposed that Rosicrucian Editions order still another work by Lama Anagarika Govinda about Tibetan Wisdom entitled *The Way of White Clouds*. It is about the pilgrimage of a Buddhist monk in Tibet. This book, which reads like a novel, enchanted the slow evenings during my stay in India. I certainly know from long experience that our teachings in the Western Tradition are irreplaceable, and they are entirely sufficient for an assured interior accomplishment that is well adapted to our times and milieu. But the readings I have carefully chosen can be aids on the path of accomplishment. They don't mean that you have to follow the precepts or be tempted by principles or experiences. That would be a mistake and probably a waste of time. Nonetheless, these works, considered as information, offer a real and efficient encouragement.

Far later than the Hindu religion, the Muslims, with their 10% of the population, came to India. I won't write at any length on what that means, intending to come back to Islam in a later special *Letter from Nowhere,* in which I will tell you about some of my former spiritual experiences in several Muslim countries. In India, Islam arrived late, with the seventh century invasions. Like Christianity, this religion insists on a society without castes. Its success with the Indians has been somewhat greater than Christianity's. I can tell you, though, that the Indians don't hide their admiration for the Muslim religion, which is naturally not to say that they are disposed to convert! There are many mosques in India, some of them quite beautiful, as there are some splendid churches. Nothing surprising about that. We have seen that this country is open to everything in the domain of the sacred without losing its own uniqueness.

Muslim mysticism, known under the name Sufism, exists in India as it does elsewhere, and I had access to it at the highest level, if I may say so, in referring in that regard to the spiritual results of a simple meeting. On the 27th of September, as a matter of fact, in Ajmer, we visited the mosque and tomb of the great Muslim saint, Sufi Khwaja-Muinud Din Chisti. Few tourists practically ever visit Ajmer, but many Indian Muslims go on pilgrimage there. The room where the tomb is located is lighted only by torches. Incense burns night and day, and fresh flowers are constantly put on the tomb. Sufis, as is their custom, were seated nearby, and were swinging back and forth while chanting their dikr, a true mantra of the sacred name of Allah. We meditated for a long time in front of the tomb, and the Indians, who when we went in thought we were just curious tourists, then crowded around us with understanding and sympathy. They felt that we considered ourselves, in reality, as their spiritual brothers, united with them that day in a holy communion. The miracle of unity of intention and of purpose was thus accomplished in a few moments, beyond the false distinctions of race, nationality, and belief.

Following that, in another room in the mosque where we had been led by the Imam, we conversed with some Muslims responsible for special services. I asked about Sufi activities in that region. While tea with milk was politely served, a servant got a discrete order, and returned with two books on *The Five Great Sufi Sages of India*. These books, although in English, are not currently available, and they presented a very great interest to me. I was happy to be able to take them back to France, regretting that I had been unable to interview the author, who was away from Ajmer that day. But we were able to visit, in his home, an aged Imam, himself a Sage, more than ninety years old, who was dying of an incurable disease.

All these contacts were accomplished by subjective impressions and experiences, during the course of which a veil was lifted. Beyond words and physical comportment, there is, every time, a communion that establishes itself on a level where beings, and even the walls we are within, disappear, and all is light. This same thing kept occurring throughout our long visit. Our itinerary had been based, of course, on human and geographic particulars, but the fact was brought back to me a thousand times that in the great Elsewhere, there was another itinerary, a mystical one, integrated with ours, and without knowing it—what would it matter, elsewhere, whether we knew it or not?—we were coming under beneficial and exalting influences. It was in that and by that, that our trip assumed its reality, its reason for being. It became a pilgrimage of light. We had no other contacts with Islam in India, but that which we did have was sufficient to satisfy the aspiration of our souls and the currents that converged in that country, because they had to include everything, not omitting the wisdom of the Muslim world, access to which, moreover, I had had so many times elsewhere.

I'll spend a little more time on Sikhism, for even though it represents only 1.7% of the population of India, it plays a large role. We didn't notice until the end of our trip, however, that Sikhism could be attractive to foreigners. It was at the airport in Delhi, on the night of our return to France, that we learned all about it. Dozens of young Americans, boys and girls were there, dressed in the splendid garments peculiar to Sikhs. They were on their way home after having come to participate in the five-hundredth anniversary of the founding of their religion. I recall being extremely impressed by Sikhism and the Sikhs. That religion is of a great nobility that is reflected on the faithful by its principles. I will one day write at greater length on that religion's philosophy, since I have been able to gather some interesting documents and fascinating information. I'm sure that you, as well as my companion and I, would have loved the luminous ambience and the freely accepted discipline of this religion, which is big, not in numbers, but in its nobility and virtue.

Generally, the great religions pride themselves in their antiquity, presenting it as an essential proof of their authenticity. Sikhism asserts that this relatively recent religion is, because of this fact, justified in its present ceaseless value. It declares itself to be the religion of our age, and when you know the universal principles behind it, you'll understand why the Sikhs hold this opinion. At least, you'll have to admit that they have the right to think this way. Today I'll give only a few pieces of general information, but, as I said, I'll return to this important subject later in another *Letter from Nowhere,* sure that you will be highly interested.

It was only in the 15th century that Sikhism got started. Its roots, however, go back to Hinduism, and it forms a mid-point between Hinduism and Islam. Its founder was Guru Nanak who, moved by a violent repulsion toward hypocrisy and swindles in religion, decided to create a new community according to reformed principles that are truer and purer. In reality, all he did was set up the basic principles, and it was in the 17th century that Sikhism, under the direction of Guru Gobind Singh, took its definite form, a religion of strict and martial conduct. They are easy to remember. The first is *kesh;* it has to do with hair, a sign of strength and virility. It is never cut. The Sikhs wear their hair in a chignon on top of the head. With children and adolescents, it is hidden and protected under a little white bonnet that holds it tight, and there is absolutely nothing ridiculous about it. The Sikhs nearly form a separate race. They are all handsome and have a virile nobility, of a sort that none of them will consent to smile or laugh. As for the adults, to hide their chignons they wear turbans of many colors, all wound identically by everyone, which adds to their natural elegance. Their hair, arranged on top of their heads, is held in place by a small comb, which constitutes the second symbol of Sikhism. This comb is called *kankha. Kara,* the third symbol, is a steel bracelet, a sign of prudence. A small dagger that serves as protection, and that is called a *kirpan,* is the fourth symbol. The fifth and last is *kacha.* That's what the short pants that are worn under their traditional garb are called. All the Sikhs are named Singh, and that's how you can recognize them. It goes without saying that you must never call a Sikh Mr. Singh. You have to use their first names. However, the Sikh who served as our guide and whom we found so often amusing, was introduced to us as Mr. Singh, and that's what we called him. Doubtless, that was for him, as it must be for others, an excellent means of keeping his anonymity.

The whole Sikh religion turns around a sacred book, The Great Saheb, which contains the fundamental principles and precepts of Sikhism. The book itself is a symbol that is highly venerated and that contains the basis of the religion. In Amritsar (which means Bowl of Nectar) you find the Golden Temple (Darbar Sahib), which is the heart of the Sikh religion and a pilgrimage center. The temple has an immense ornamental lake in front of it, surrounded by white marble pillars, and to get to the temple you pass over a marble bridge. In that place only silence and peace reign and all the vibratory ambience seems to emanate from the cosmic prana. The Sikhs really commune with that environment, and they do it, so to speak, physically, because they believe that they can obtain divine nourishment that permits them to triumph over sickness, doubt, or even death. You enter that holy place after taking your shoes off, just as you do in a mosque, and you are given houseslippers, for free. As a matter of fact, no gift is accepted. Even foreign visitors are not permitted to enter if they are bareheaded. You have to wear a turban, or at least a scarf big enough to cover your head. In the sanctuary under a canopy sits the Great Saheb, the Holy Book. It is wrapped in several sumptuous scarves strewn with sweet-smelling flowers, and seated before it is a majestic Sikh, dressed all in white, even his turban, wearing a beard, like all Sikhs, cross-legged on the floor. On his right behind some balustrades or railings, some musicians are playing on a small portable reed organ, accompanying the vaulting recitative of the chanters, while on his left and behind him, separated from the choir by railings, some Sikhs are meditating, also sitting cross-legged on the floor, moving their bodies to the rhythm of the chants. We followed the crowd of pilgrims, saluted the Great Saheb, received communion—a ball of bread—and we meditated at length among the Sikhs. Then on the second floor of the marble building, very moved, we saw and heard other venerable Sikhs chanting, each in a bare room with a Holy Book before them, and from an interior balcony we glanced up at the sanctuary where the service was going on, a service that begins at four in the morning and doesn't end until ten in the evening.

That same evening, we got back in time to witness the retreat of the Great Saheb. A litter borne on the shoulders of Sikhs approached on the marble bridge. It was followed by the crowd. A Sikh shouting some ritual words preceded the cortege. The venerable old man, who at that moment was the guardian of the Book, got up, and slowly and solemnly some helpers removed the five scarves that covered the Great Saheb. He placed the Book on his head and walked outside toward the litter, and with great respect he placed the Book on the litter, and the procession began amid prayers and chants. When the cortege reached the end of the bridge the powerful sound of an immense drum beaten with two clubs came out of another building. That's where the Holy Book was slowly carried and set with veneration on the bed where it would remain until, with solemnity, it would be brought back to the Sikh service, after which, during the interval, the sanctuary would be carefully cleaned. We followed all this ceremony from close up, participating in all of its phases, and we had the privilege of being among those who were able to attend the arrival of the Book at the room where it was kept. I have rarely seen such a moving and impressive, symbolic, and grandiose ceremony in a religious service. It exalted us through an exceptional experience that culminated in the penetrating sound of the drum that marked a flight toward sublime spheres.

Around the sacred pool and in a big near-by building pilgrims coming from far-off lands, and even foreigners, can stay for three days for free. Furthermore, free meals are prepared every day in the huge kitchens of another building for a large number of unfortunates or visitors. They often prepare more than 10,000 meals at a time! Near the pool is the Akal Takht, the immortal throne that contains several relics and the seat of the supreme authority of Sikhism. Everything in that holy place is impregnated with a rare beauty and an energy that is the very essence of the soul of the Sikhs. We got a similar impression later on the 15th of October in Patna, where the tenth and last guru of the Sikhs was born, at the superb temple of that noble religion. But I'll always remember the visit to that temple for another reason. We had walked onto a magnificent marble terrace that overlooks the city. In the distance the sun was setting.

The next morning we were to leave for Bodh-Gaya, which is the cradle and Mecca of Buddhism, and is unfortunately never included in tourists' itineraries. However, that is where Gautama Buddha received his great Illumination seated under the Bo tree. But, suddenly, there on the terrace of the Sikh temple where we were watching the sunset, and without in any way being able to predict such an experience, without thinking, I raised my eyes toward the sun, and for a long moment I saw the Buddha in the sun, seated in that universally-known posture. Was I, in spite of it all, in a particular inner state necessary for this kind of experience? I can't say, but in any case I was objectively conscious enough to say to my friend "Look at the sun!" and I believe that he too saw a peculiar shape, without sharing my sublime experience. My whole trip was filled with similar and different experiences. Presently I will talk about some of them unreservedly, as I have already done elsewhere.

Jainism (.05% of the population) is the most moving religion that could exist on earth. It is peculiar to western India. In appearance, solely in appearance, naturally, the Jains don't seem to be preoccupied with supernatural matters. Their beliefs are essentially on the philosophical level. The two principles of Jainism are non-violence, understood and observed in the most absolute sense, and tolerance, a tolerance based on understanding and benevolence toward all other beliefs whatever they are. For the Jains, right science, conduct, faith, and chastity bring health, and what they mean by right conduct is found in the two principles just introduced.

Humankind, according to Jainism, must free itself from the energy of matter, because that is separate and distinct from the soul. Those who reach that point are not gods. They are perfect souls that should be considered as examples, as Sages that the Jains call tirthankarars. So the Jains are not in quest of a god who is the creator of the universe. That god is eternal. He exists in himself. The goal is the deliverance of the soul. It must be freed from material ties. A little after our arrival in India, in Bombay, on the 21st of September, we visited a Jain temple. There all is calm, silence, and peace, reflecting the very essence of that religion's high principles. On the ground floor in little chapels, as well as on the second floor, statues receive the homage of the faithful, homage but not ceremony. Those statues represent the Sages, the Fulfilled, the tirthankaras. Before them incense is burnt, flowers and rice are offered. Only the monks are admitted to the interior of the chapels to take care of the statues and to show a very special veneration to that which they represent. Ordinary Jains, and even more foreign strangers, are allowed only into the temple itself. For everybody, however, it is possible to meditate intensely and to feel a sublime communion. That's what my companion and I didn't forget to do, during the first hours of our long visit, since it was by contact with Jainism that everything began for us.

Among the Jains the principle of non-violence is pushed to the extreme, I learned. It is well known that in order to avoid accidentally killing a minute insect while breathing, many Jains wear a veil on their faces. One of our guides explained to us how far this respect for life can go among the Jains. He told us about a friendly family living nearby. In order not to crush or wound any insect inadvertently, they never go out after dark. That certainly seems to be pushing things a bit too far in respecting a principle. But nobody should condemn such an attitude. This principle of the respect for life is alive, and non-violence is admirable, because in this regard, as in many others, one exception will engender new exceptions, and that's how a rule gets to be ignored and forgotten. In our world of verbal and physical violence, don't we wish that a few little seeds of Jainism could sprout?

The last religion of any importance in India is Zoroastrianism, whose members are called Parsis. These people, fleeing Muslim persecutions in their native Persia, arrived in India in the 7th century, and they were established especially in Bombay and in nearby areas. They follow a path called Asha, that is to say, a line of conduct based on good thoughts, words, and actions. Their holy book is the Zend Avesta which describes the eternal fight between Ormuzd and Arihman, otherwise called good and evil, and which defines the place of humankind at the heart of this conflict.

The Parsis don't accept any converts, out of respect even today, of the solemn obligation, taken in the year 720 A.D. before the Hindu king who had welcomed them to his territory, not to proselytize. They respect their promise made in India so much that no one can visit their temples there, but it is possible to do so in Iran. It is useful to have a good knowledge of Zoroastrianism. This religion is related to that of the Vedic Hindus. Its adepts, as a matter of fact, venerate but do not adore, as is too often believed, fire and other natural elements. The sun and fire are, for the Paris, the appropriate symbols of God All Powerful, because He is splendor, light, and glory. Evidently, after twelve centuries of proximity with the Hindus, the Zoroastrians had come to resemble them in their customs, and that's what explains the efforts over the last century to take this religion back to its pure origins, those of the original Zend Avesta.

It is because fire is sacred to them that the Parsis, in order not to dishonor themselves, do not cremate their dead. Neither do they bury them, because the earth is also sacred to them. So, what do they do? Sensitive people might be horrified to learn about their customs, but taking everything into account, we had better have another look. The dead are carried to a big field where they are put in simple cottages where for two days rites and services are carried out for them. Then the bodies are taken by special workers to the Towers of Silence. In these, there are three levels, those for men, women, and children. The bodies are then devoured by vultures. Neither the fields nor the towers can be visited. At our request, however, our guide asked our driver to go by one of these fields near Bombay. We saw nothing but a big vulture on a palm tree nearby, feeding its hungry young in a nest, and we accepted these facts. Our guide was a young Parsi woman, graceful, beautiful, full of culture and refinement. I couldn't help thinking of the fate of her physical self, such a beautiful expression of a soul. But, after all, what does it matter what happens to a useless body? And that evening, talking with a young Parsi named Ormuzd who demonstrated again to me the misery of India by pointing out young students who, not having reading lamps at home, simply because they could not afford to pay for electricity, were studying on the steps of a public building by the light of street lamps. I couldn't help thinking that one day his lifeless corpse would be food for vultures.

The Parsis, on the other hand, were the first in India to adopt Western customs and education. Furthermore, they are very forward looking, and nearly all of them are in business. It is among these people, comprising only .03% of the population, that you find the richest, by far. And if they are unique in India as a rich group of people, they are also known as the most generous. When you travel in India you will often see the name Tata, the name of prosperity. Trucks, factories, banks, commercial centers have this name. Mr. Tata is a Parsi, and one day soon he will be put out to pasture for the vultures.

Such are the principal religions of India: Hinduism, as we have kept on insisting, is the most important. I went to India not to observe, but to participate with the greatest respect in all of those important traditions, and it was so that my companion entered into our research. So it was that when we were with the Parsis, we were Parsis, with the Jains we were Jains, with the Sikhs we were Sikhs, and with the Hindus we were Hindu. As we will soon see, when the time comes, we were Buddhists with the Buddhists. I could tell the people we were with, without being dishonest in any way, that when I was there among them I belonged to their religions. When we visited their temples or joined in their ceremonies, it was so at those moments. Placing myself by means of initiation at the level of primordial unity, I clothed myself for a time in an aspect of its realization in diversity, and I was completely caught up in that aspect with absolute sincerity.

The Hindus are strict vegetarians, and so we were ourselves most of the time. The vegetarian food in India is excellent, especially the famous vegetable cutlets. I might mention here that the Buddhists, in particular the Tibetans, are not vegetarians. It is the Hindus who are strictest in this regard. It is true that they believe in the transmigration of souls, including the possibility of their return, if such is their karma, in the bodies of animals or even insects. I had had to kill a few mosquitos that were bothering me while I was steeping myself in Hinduism's spiritual aspects, and it led me to think a bit about killing. I was quite upset about those murders that I committed. I kept asking my Hindu friends everywhere "So is it possible that my soul, for example, will come back in a mosquito?" Invariably, they replied "It's possible!" Every time, I tried to argue this way: "But if I kill a mosquito, basically, I'm doing it's soul a favor! It surely can't be fun to be a mosquito. I'm just giving its soul the possibility of a quicker and better reincarnation when I snuff out its life!" A few of my Hindu friends would answer, perhaps out of politeness, having decided that I hadn't understood anything at all: "It's evidently a point of view to consider that I've never really given much thought!" But others, unhappily, were not quite so encouraging: "Maybe for the mosquito that's finally a good thing. However, for you, there is karma because you have committed a bad deed. As a matter of fact, killing is forbidden." In spite of all that, I kept on killing mosquitos, but with greater regret than before, while murmuring with less and less conviction as I committed my crimes what I always said (was this just to appease my conscience?): "God's tiny creature, I'm sending you to the cosmic world, where you will find more joy and beauty in your physical form in the future!" I confess to having omitted saying these healing words from time to time. I've gone back to my old habits. Mosquitos always bite. My skin is sensitive. What would you do in my situation?

It is this same belief that explains the Hindu attitude toward cows, even though in addition there are other, deeper, philosophical reasons, but I'll spare you the difficult explanations. There is even a logical reason that is a lot easier to understand, and we owe it to the head of our travel agency in Udaipur where we arrived on the 24th of September. After having declared like any good Hindu that all ways lead to the same God, in answer to my question about sacred cows he said: "In India, nobody will allow cows to lose their sacred character. Unsuccessfully, the government issued an edict on this subject. They retracted it quickly because the revolt against it rose everywhere. Our wise ancestors were right to give the cows their privileges in declaring them to be sacred. There is such great misery in our country, and the cows produce essential food—milk—and everything that comes from it: cheese, butter, etc. Moreover, they give birth to the males, which are used for traction when they grow up. And finally, they provide the dung that we use as fertilizer, and also as fuel in cold regions. It is used everywhere in the countryside as construction material." What he told us in such a haughty tone of voice is true. Without the products of the cows there would be no solution to the misery of India and famine would attain tragic proportions. After molding the dung into the shape of slabs, they stick it onto walls in new construction, and for repairs. Without dung, a lot of people in the countryside wouldn't have a roof to live and sleep under.

For that matter, it might surprise you to learn that the cows in India are not at all the walking skeletons that are often represented in photo magazines. There are a few like that, especially in the cities, for example in Calcutta, where they interfere with the already difficult traffic situation that the Indians seem to put up with quite well. Cows don't find much to eat in the cities. But most of the cows do quite well elsewhere, and so they are fat. In the small villages and the countryside generally, every morning they return unerringly to their individual owners for milking and rest. In some regions, particularly in the South, they are used by non-Hindus as draft animals, to pull a plow or a cart. I'm not sure this makes Hindus very happy. Anyway, they look the other way, probably because in those regions they are in the minority relative to the Muslims. Everywhere else, cows have a free and happy life. Rather than coming back to earth as a mosquito, if you have the choice, I would suggest coming back as a sacred cow. I often said that to my friend, and he always agreed. I suppose that the cow's elegance comes from its horns. They come in a surprising variety of shapes. Besides, every year there is a cow festival. The horns are painted red or blue, or both, or other colors, and the color stays on the horns all year. It's a nice custom. Since almost everywhere the cows don't have to do anything, it is the bulls and the buffaloes that are used as traction animals. Oh, the buffaloes! You see them everywhere. When they aren't working, they prefer to stay in the water. You see their magnificent heads in the rivers, the lakes, the ponds, their bodies under the water, in an impressive immobility. Their owners have a hard time getting them out of the water because they do not at all prefer the heat. And for the birds, they are everywhere, and it is the same for the animals. India is their paradise, because the people respect their lives, since they have a strong belief in the transmigration of souls. A foreign visitor must be taken aback in seeing so many animals in freedom, the birds everywhere, the little amphibians and mammals given complete freedom. Each morning, the birds, in their brilliant plumage, give out their songs of joy and happiness. It is strange to see little animals, squirrels, for example, treated like guests—the rarest and the most common. The Indians don't seem to be afraid of any of the so-called inferior species. Of course they know that certain birds and animals, notably a kind of monkey, are irascible. As for them, that's the way they are and the Indians take it into account. Furthermore, the best way to get along together is to leave them alone—birds, animals, and even snakes (even the cobra is sacred and respected). So the Indians believe that they won't be attacked by any animal whatsoever. Animals are part of their lives and their surroundings, and so they don't worry about them.

In the next *Letter from Nowhere* I'll tell you in particular about the ashrams in India and about certain gurus or instructors. It is only after looking into this subject that I'll take up Buddhism, more particularly Tibetan Buddhism. As a matter of fact, in Dharamsala and Sikkim I met some grand Lamas as well as some exiled Tibetans, and we held many exciting conversations. I didn't miss any exceptional encounters or experiences, and I believe you will be captivated by what I learned about the Master Maitreya, the future Buddha whom everybody out there is waiting for, and who, according to them, will come from the West.

Very sincerely yours,
Raymond Bernard

6

APRIL 1978

Secret Ashrams

Dear Friends,

At the beginning of last December I had written exactly three pages of this *Letter from Nowhere*. Certainly, if I had been able to get it finished in December as I had planned, this sixth *Letter from Nowhere* would have been printed and sent out in time. But that wasn't the case, for on the 8th of December I was at the Chateau d' Omonville where I had a myocardial infarction when I woke up that morning. Then I had to put up with the guilty incompetence of a doctor in Neubourg who misdiagnosed the heart attack and its severity. And to make it all worse, he waited ten hours—from eight in the morning to six in the evening—before sending me to a colleague (after repeated, anguished telephone calls from my wife) who then, in order to justify the first doctor's decisions, lied about the seriousness of the heart attack. Following bad advice, I went to that cardiologist in Evreux by car. I should have gone by ambulance that very morning after my doctor had given me something for the intolerable and indescribable pain in my chest that lasted half a day without medical care. Moreover, during that same day, trying to conquer the pain, in a physical state of complete distress, I read the proof sheets of the preceding *Letter from Nowhere*, number five.

In relating such personal news in such detail in this letter, I do so because in a later letter I intend to come back to the subject of the sickness that befell me. I'll do this, not because the subject is interesting in itself, but only because then I'll be able to take up the subject of health in general in this world that we live in. In our existence we often have to put up with a dangerous environment full of pollution. In treating this subject, I'll explain to you that the hour of death, rather than being otherwise absolutely fixed, as I had written in a chapter of one of my books, is no less perfectly determined by karmic causes that we establish in this or earlier lives. These are what permit us to say metaphorically that the moment of death is fixed in an existence determined by an inescapable cosmic decree. A whole *Letter from Nowhere* will be devoted to this important subject, and it will doubtless enlighten you on obscure points while reinforcing your admiration of the grandeur and beauty of the cosmic laws.

In the meantime, I trust I will be permitted to divulge here something that my family and friends are well aware of. I had a premonition for months before my heart attack that it was going to happen. Since the month of June, 1977, I had been meaning to consult a cardiologist because of certain symptoms I had. I didn't do it, I suppose, because I felt that the doctor would make me cancel my planned trip to India, and I felt that I couldn't do that, no matter what, because of the importance of this pilgrimage to our sources. Even in India, on two occasions, I felt the symptoms return, but I paid no attention to them. It is possible, even though I doubt it, that certain unfavorable forces had tried to impede my trip. Anyway, things could have been even more difficult, but they could not have been changed or delayed in any way. Besides, I prefer another explanation. Certain important events in our lives are programmed, and we can't change anything for the simple reason that they have to teach us a big lesson. My deep conviction, I could even say my certainty, is the case with the heart attack I had. Actually, on my return from India, after some tests I asked for, having consulted a doctor in Villeneuve Saint-Georges on the 5th of December, and telling him about my symptoms, he said it was nothing serious, but that I should see a cardiologist. The first one I telephoned couldn't see me until the following Thursday, but one of his colleagues could see me on Saturday, so I chose that date. On the 6th of December I went back to the Chateau d'Omonville, and I had the attack on the 8th. So it is not possible to doubt that this event was fully programmed into my life! Also, for 72 days—one half of the mystical number 144—I was first in a clinic in Evreux and then at the well-known cardiology center at Evecquemont, in the department of Yvelines. There I had experiences and encounters of a powerful human interest that I'll tell you about later.

There is one person out there among you who told me that he was never worried—my travelling companion. He had heard an important guru who had received us state that I would die at the age of 89 years! I heard that too, but age 89, that sounds too much for me, even if my father lived longer! But my companion's confidence gave me great pleasure, reminding me of moments during a trip heavy with important consequences, moments when we felt a need for relaxation.

And so today I'm writing this sixth *Letter from Nowhere.* I'm working in a convalescent home located in Combloux, near Megève. Curiously, among the etymologies of the name Combloux, there is one that makes sense of the nearby forests, and that I like very much: Combloux comes from Cumba Loci, the valley of the sacred wood where the druid ceremonies were held. This place gives off vibrations of a strange mystical significance. Also, the view from here is like no other. From my room, in front of a large bay window where I write, you can see Mont Blanc, which seems to be near and distant at the same time, standing there in immaculate whiteness and imposing grandeur, shining beneath the sun, while clouds fade away. My wife, in her discrete devotion and inspired by mystical, silent, reserved goodness, chose this place of beauty, harmony and peace for me. And suddenly it seems that I am back in Sikkim at Gangtok, and even nearer than Gangtok stand the white peaks of the Himalayas. There is no coincidence in the world. Everything here creates a well-known ambience for me, and so I am able to get back to work on the subject of this *Letter from Nowhere* more easily, taking up where I left off in December, when I was interrupted by the temporary failure of a heart that is often knowingly overworked.

Today we will speak again about India. In the two preceding letters we examined this grand country, first its geography, its society, and even by innuendo its politics. Then we concentrated our attention on the religious environment that conditions the Indian people both in their interior lives as well as in their comportment and daily existence. In this *Letter from Nowhere* I propose to treat the subject of the ashrams of India, that is to say, the communities where disciples are assembled around a guru or instructor, or where they perpetuate his memory and his teachings. These ashrams are of a significant number. I was going to write considerable, but their importance varies, at least according to our Western understanding. I certainly couldn't discuss all of them! In order to do that I would have to draw up a general plan and spend years in India. I'm convinced, furthermore, that if that were the case, such a plan would still be incomplete because some groups that in every respect deserve to be called ashrams consist only of one guru and a few disciples, and they are often the most authentic.

At Trivandrum my companion and I had an exceptional guide. His opinion on this subject is worth quoting. Here it is: "The ashrams, when they become big and too important, lose the purity of purpose that they originally had. Inevitable material preoccupations dilute the work of their founders. At the beginning and even during his whole life, the guru has only one concern—that of dispensing his teachings and transmitting his wisdom. When he is no longer there, the soul and the heart of the ashram dissolve, leaving only the material aspects. That is perhaps necessary for the message to be widely disseminated, but it's too bad. It is born, it lives, and it dies..." Each of us can understand that a community dependent upon a single man, even if that man is a sage or a guru, can survive no longer than that man. When he is gone, the community necessarily changes its nature, which doesn't mean, in my opinion—and here I disagree with my guide—that it does no useful work, on the contrary. What is necessary to remember, anyway, is the respect that the Indians pay toward the ashrams. How could it be otherwise? Here are people whose lives are filled with religion, and who base their entire existence on a daily mystical quest, even if this quest is apparently shrouded with material aspects. That is something that regular tourists don't take into account. They are really not interested, and they are concerned with the countryside and monuments. To understand fully the importance of ashrams in India it is necessary to emphasize the intensity of the religious life of this country through some examples. To this end I will share with you a few significant facts that I was able to gather personally.

The Hindu temples and sanctuaries number into the thousands. They are visited by millions of pilgrims. However, they are not the principal center of the religion. Actually, the Hindus stay in the temples only a few minutes for a brief visit to their chosen divinity, and some of them never go. It is at home in the family chapel before their altar that the Hindus perform their religious duties. This is so fundamental to them that I do not hesitate to repeat it to emphasize the point. When they get up in the morning, each member of the family, father, mother, and children, most often individually, but on special occasions all together, goes to the family chapel, after bathing. There, before the altar and the chosen divinity (the god that they have selected) everyone prostrates himself, his forehead against the floor, then he joins his hands together and prays or recites a mantra or a passage from the Holy Writings of Hinduism. If there is enough time, every Hindu stays at least ten minutes in his chapel. In Benares, since we were leaving at an early hour for Allahabad, I asked our guide whether he had had the time, before joining us at our hotel at five o'clock, to go through his daily practice. "Naturally," he answered, "but I remained at the altar for only a few minutes, before excusing myself. I have to do that sometimes, because of my work obligations, but later I'll stay longer in the family chapel. And not to go there at all, even one day, never!" And before the car left, he prayed silently, asking for our protection on the trip and a benediction on all of us. Of course, we joined in with all our heart.

The Hindu goes into his chapel in the evening too before going to bed, and he wouldn't forget to do this anymore than he would in the morning. This same spiritual habit is found all over Asia among the Buddhists. For example, in Japan, in nearly every town there is a street devoted to selling religious articles for family chapels. In Tokyo I saw very beautiful furniture for chapels, at all prices, even for modest budgets. When the Hindu, like the Buddhist, builds a house or furnishes an apartment, he thinks first of the location of his altar, and if there isn't much room, the greater part of it will nonetheless be reserved for his family chapel. I will presently tell you about the emotion I felt this subject when we visited the home of a poor Tibetan. That experience will always remain engraved in our memory and our heart.

The religious comportment of the Hindus and Buddhists is such that whenever they encounter a temple—even if it is nothing but ruins or unique and impressive vestiges like those of Ellora or of Ajanta dug into the flank of a mountain from top to bottom—they immediately pray, or meditate, and they give an offering—a simple flower or a coin. They behave this way even in museums. In the Buddhist section of the Karachi Museum, in Pakistan in August, 1975, I saw a Japanese seated in prayer before a statue of the Buddha. He remained in that position for a long time without the other visitors bothering him in any way. He was surrounded by everyone's discretion and respect.

Without neglecting the twice-daily worship, and even more often during critical times, the Hindu doesn't forget to participate in the Puja (public ceremonies), and he does everything possible to go on a pilgrimage to a major center at least once during his life.

The most religious city in India is incontestably Varanasi, formerly known as Benares. It is the City of Death, because for a Hindu to die in Varanasi is both a privilege and a blessing. In the 7th century B.C. this unique city already existed, and was called Kasi, the meaning of which, That Shines with Divine Light, is significant. Varanasi, or if you prefer, Benares, is in any case one of the oldest cities on earth. It is also the cradle of secular traditions. Every Hindu tries to go there at least once in his life, and if possible to die there. The Ganges—Ganga, the Hindu name—is the heart of the religious life there. This sacred river is venerated all along its banks, from its source to the sea. Its water is said to be beneficial and curative. At Hardwar, for example, near the Himalayas, in the cold water of the young, fresh river, we saw several Hindus in prayer, but Varanasi is the main sanctuary of this holy river. There is a repulsive squalor in that city. At the place where a large number of cremations are done, the corpses are first plunged into the river. Corpses tied to stones are sometimes immersed in the river. Cadavers of animals can be seen floating on the water. People bathe in the Ganges, sewers empty into it, but nonetheless careful medical analyses show that the water of the Ganges is bacteriologically pure. When you think about the river and what it carries, you are certainly tempted to proclaim a miracle! A Hindu remarked to me that so many new bacteria are always being poured into the river that they must certainly wipe out the bacteria that are already there. That's an explanation, even if I ignore the scientific value of it, but the fact is there, though incomprehensible and without a believable explanation, unless the vibrations created in those places by constructive and benevolent thoughts every day for thousands of years have the power of purification. And I'm tempted to admit it, because if the solution to a problem can't be found through usual reasoning, I look freely in a domain that is much more vast.

My companion and I got up one morning to see the sunrise over the Ganges. We went along the river in a boat. There, thousands of Hindus in the river, facing the sun, performed their worship service. The spectacle is grandiose, indescribable. You have to have been there in order to relive it in your thoughts and understand it. At the moment the sun appeared we all fell silent, and eyes closed, we united our prayers and meditations with those of the immense crowd of people that heard and saw nothing but their devotions. And even the logs of the Manikarnita ghat where the corpses of the dead were burning, and from which rose a thick cloud of smoke, did not seem repulsive to us when our boat drew near them and when, and this happens rarely because the pyres are arranged in a manner to avoid such an incident, a blackened corpse half rose out of the ardent flames. That evening we returned to the Ganges, and seated near the river, we meditated at length. Then in homage we threw into the river the flowers we had just bought for that purpose. They floated away, carried along by the current, among tiny candles put in the water by the faithful as a sign of veneration. In leaving, we stopped near one of the numerous parasols that the Brahmans sit under, and for a small offering one of them blessed us. Then I asked whether the very old woman, so thin in the big sari that she clasped around her, who the night before was found sitting and then lying on a large stone, waiting for death, had quit this vale of tears. Like so many others, she had probably asked to be brought there to die, or her loved ones had brought her there in spite of her wishes, so that her anguish not be prolonged.

Varanasi has innumerable holy places, and the whole city is a unique sanctuary. There is that of Shiva, whose worship, perhaps the very oldest, has been carried out for thousands of years. One of Shiva's wives, Sati, was thrown onto his funeral pyre in order to honor him, and until the 19th century the Hindus kept on doing this to widows until the British put an end to this barbaric rite!

In India, Varanasi is not the only holy place, but it is no doubt the most important one among many others. There are many others that resemble Varanasi in the sorts of worship practiced there, too many to be concerned with here. But I'll tell you about Allahabad, a city that I have already alluded to. As I observed before, no foreign tourists go there. I had looked forward to visiting it as part of our itinerary, and at this point I can assure you that again my companion and I slipped into a vast mystical gathering. It was as if every step was chosen by reason of geography, while in reality it was forces from on high which inspired and dictated what we were to do. They gave our trip its spiritual aura that we were seeking. Since there is no tourist activity in Allahabad, the only hotel, Barnet's Hotel, is perhaps the least comfortable in the world. We did not sleep well there, but that didn't prevent us from getting a very rich experience from that holy city. It is there in Allahabad that you find the underground temples of Fort Akbar. Only the Indians know about it, and only the Hindus worship the numerous divinities of that vast underground complex. Near there you can find the temple of the Sleeping Hanuman. With our guide we paid homage to the representation of the monkey-god, but again, among the crowd of believers, we were the only two foreigners.

That same evening, the 11th of October, on a road going to our hotel, I had the car stop in front of an ashram that I spotted. That ashram is known as Bharat Sevashram Sangha. We spoke at length with the leader of the community, and shortly afterwards we were given the privilege, as no other strangers ever had, of visiting the temple and meditating in its impressive, vibratory ambience. This ashram, whose guru was deceased, is governed by extremely hard rules that seemed to me nearly sectarian. It has affiliates in different cities, and it supports charitable activities there, like most such communities in India. But I don't think that such an ashram can help many people. We saw only Indians there, and they all seemed to be bound by rigid rules.

As I told you in an earlier letter, the Indians are not very sympathetic toward strangers even though they show them the greatest courtesy. But with us, everyone we approached seemed to bend over backwards to accommodate us, and even went to great lengths to make sure that we became their friends. So it was in Allahabad one evening that our guide took us to visit his wealthy relatives who owned a fabric store with some twenty employees. There we met one of our guide's relatives, the violinist, who threw much light on Indian life for us. He took us to a conference on the Bhagavad-Gita given by an eminent Swami, Chitayananda. It had been publicized and announced all over the city. The hall was packed, and other conferences were to follow the one we attended. The Swami was seated on the stage in the lotus position, and his long discourse in English was peppered with colorful remarks that he laughed at himself. All the Indians present seemed to appreciate the Swami's remarks to the highest degree. And I wondered whether in our countries of false modesty and prudishness, where everything sacred can only be transmitted in a stiff, formal manner, the Swami's inspired message could have been understood.

The next day, the 12th of October, was a great day of mystical communion for me and my companion. As arranged with our guide we were ready at five-thirty in the morning. Our driver was there already, for he had slept in the car. It was the guide who was missing. The violinist, with whom the guide lived, offered us morning tea to keep us occupied while we waited. From his home we had an exceptional view of Allahabad.

Finally we were ready to go. Another car followed ours. Our guide's aged mother and her daughter, a widow, were in it. We went toward the river. On the boat that our guide had reserved for us, his mother and sister sat across from him, preparing and filling small receptacles. The boat drifted slowly toward the confluence of India's three greatest sacred rivers: the Ganges, the

Yamana, and the mystical Sarasvati, which passes under Fort Akbar, near the subterranean temples, to join the other two. There were thousands and thousands of pilgrims because that day throughout India the festivals of the goddess Durga, the wife of Vishnu, were beginning. It was also by coincidence the last day of the festival of the ancestors. After drifting a long distance we arrived at the point of confluence of the three sacred rivers, which all together have a considerable width. The boat stopped exactly in the middle. There was a strong current, but curiously we stayed still. The water was warm. As a sign of purification, my companion and I bathed in the river for a long time, like the other pilgrims. Other boats were there, coming and going. Everything was taking place with good humor, joy and laughter. What an example these eminently religious people gave us! Finally we got back in the boat, and drying ourselves, we took the receptacles that our guide's mother handed to us, and after presenting them to the sun, we threw into the water a little milk, some water, seeds, and flower petals. This puja, or ceremony, was very moving. I think that over the thousands of years it has been practiced, up until now my companion and I are the only non-Hindus to participate in it. You can understand, my dear friends, what we must have felt.

On our return to Varanasi, we went once again to the ashram of Ma Ananda Moy. We had already gone there on the 9th of October, but Ma was absent, and by the 12th she hadn't come back. She was at home, known only to her loved ones, in order to rest. Moreover, every Hindu is perfectly conscious of what burden to the physical self that a mystical or spiritual charge can be. And if he knew the place where a Sage had gone to get away from the world for a time, he would keep silent and seem to know nothing about it. On the part of the Indians, that is what we could call mystical discretion, the value of which is incontestable, since, for the initiated, to know and to be silent are two fundamental, complementary rules. Ma is now known everywhere. She is, in her perfect accomplishment, the expression of the bounty of goodness and love, a goodness and love so absolute that no contrary word, allusion, or attitude can diminish them. The way that she took and of which she is the realization is that of devotion—Bhakti Yoga. It would take volumes to tell you about Ma. Several exist in French, and if they are not out of print I'll have them ordered by Rosicrucian Editions (56, rue Gambetta, 94190 Villeneuve Saint-Georges) which will certainly have them in stock if they are reprinted. You must not miss reading them. You must get to know Ma. She is the Saint par excellence. Even if she is not there, her ashram is full of Her presence. My companion and I meditated in the little courtyard on the 9th and again on the 12th. During that last visit, Ma's chapel on the second floor was open for cleaning, and during a period when no one was there, we took the opportunity to meditate in it. During the course of that meditation I felt Ma's blessing very intensely. The ashram is situated on the banks of the Ganges. There a few years ago several mystics benefitted from a ceremony that I prepared for them. However, I wasn't able to conduct it myself, being called away on a trip at the last moment. I reminded Ma's secretary about that.

It was again at Varanasi, on that same evening of the 12th of October, that we went to the Ramakrishna Mission to attend an evening worship service and to take part in the chanting. There, in that place of peace and power, I had unbelievable experiences when I was seated among the Hindus with my companion in front of the expressive portrait of the great and holy Ramakrishna. I relived these same experiences on the 24th of October when we went to Belur Math, the international seat of the Ramakrishna Mission in Calcutta. Indeed, we stopped on our way at the temple of Kali to visit the room where Ramakrishna lived for thirty-five years and where he received his illuminations, and my companion and I both felt a powerful mystical sensation and vibrations of a particular intensity throughout our whole bodies. In addition, for me there was an added, spontaneous, mystical unfolding during which I was consciously living on two planes—

the physical, and the spiritual—which is extremely rare without preparation and practice. At that moment I was suffused throughout my being with the teachings of Ramakrishna that I had known intellectually so well for many years. Outside that holy room stands the small building where Ramakrishna's wife lived for all those years. At Belur Math, we meditated outside the room where Ramakrishna's celebrated disciple Vivekananda died, and we did the same a little farther on at the place where he was cremated.

On the 29th of October at Cape Cormorin, the southernmost point in India, we visited the ashram of Vivekananda himself, and then we went by boat to the rock where Vivekananda meditated for several days and where a vast edifice was built. This was when our guide expressed the opinions that I reported at the beginning of this *Letter from Nowhere*. Still, if you think about it, these ashrams visited by immense crowds of people and by sincere seekers have a profound reason for being, in spite of the inevitable, necessary, and even indispensable commercial aspects of the temporal existence of the community. They testify to the strength and vigor of mysticism and spirituality in a time when you might think they should have disappeared, simply because of the decline of the categorical and formalistic religions. This decline is aggravated, unfortunately, by the fact that they have not fulfilled their mission, as they were supposed to, of serving God and humanity. They have not yet found their way toward a true renewal, in spite of the laudable efforts by many individuals in their midst. Through their intolerance, sectarianism, and often fanaticism, they remain caught in a past which is long gone. The ashrams of Ramakrishna, Vivekananda, or of Sri Aurobindo, of which I will speak later, are large communities. They seem somewhat external and shallow, but you would be wrong to depend on appearances. From these ashrams have come great saints, Accomplished Ones, and from them will come even more. As rare as they are, they are testimonies to the value of the message received.

It was our guide from Trivandrum who took us to Cape Cormorin, and that guide, full of good sense and wisdom about the conduct of life, could himself become a guru and found an ashram. I told him that, and I even suggested a name to use as a guru. He didn't say he wouldn't. He had great experience.

If I wanted to go back to Trivandrum, it was because that's where Kamal Joumblatt often went and where he proposed to retire just before his assassination. Although I knew the name of his guru, who had been dead for many years, I had no idea whatsoever about the location of his ashram. Kamal Joumblatt never told me, and I never asked him. So, I had hardly any chance of finding it. But, as I have repeated so many times in these letters devoted to India, my trip involved a much greater dimension than a simple itinerary, and from On High someone was watching. Thus, at Trivandrum, as in all the other towns, a guide was waiting for us. He was having some trouble collecting our luggage, and it was growing late. He came over to me to make conversation while we were waiting, and I was seized with a sudden inspiration. I said to him, "Here in Trivandrum, there is an ashram I'd like to get to know, but I've forgotten the address. One of my Lebanese friends..." He interrupted me bluntly: "Kamal, Kamal Joumblatt," he said, "that's who you are referring to, isn't it?" If I hadn't been perceptive, I would have been astounded at this coincidence. "Yes, that's him," I answered. Then he said, "I knew Kamal Joumblatt for thirty years. Twenty-five years ago I took him to the ashram of the great Ramana Maharsi, who is now deceased. In those days my home was near the place where that Sage lived. Fifteen years later, here at Trivandrum, I saw Kamal again and became his regular guide. His ashram, the ashram of Krishna Menon, yes, I know it well. I often took him there. He wrote to me before he was assassinated, telling me that he intended to retire there. His brutal murder gave me great pain..." He explained to me that the ashram was one hundred and eighty kilometers away, and that it would take us three hours to get there. We were to spend so little time at Trivandrum that on the 29th we got up at five-thirty to go to Cape Cormorin, came back around noon, and left again at two p.m. for the ashram of Krishna Menon, arriving there after more than three hours.

On our arrival we surprised—in the strongest sense of the termathe disciples. We had to undergo a real interrogation. I told them about Kamal Joumblatt, my meetings with him, and our different conversations. After some time the disciples accepted us with more favor. They were American and French, but there were very few of them. We were shown the way to a small room they prepared for us, where we had tea. We exchanged a lot of ideas, but the three disciples who were with us were extremely discrete about the teachings and training they were receiving. Actually, the guru, son and successor of Krishna Menon, wasn't there. They were expecting him to return around six-thirty, but around six o'clock they told us that he would be returning late and he would be tired. I thought then that it was probably best to leave. Just as our car went through the gate, another car arrived and went to a house higher up the hill. It was the guru returning from his trip and it was written that we should never meet.

That ashram is a secret ashram. You can get in only by recommendation and invitation. That is the kind of ashram in India that is the most real and authentic. They are reserved for those who are ready and who have decided to sacrifice everything to come find, in silence and in secret, the truth that takes many years to acquire. A young Frenchman had been there for five years and his very being vibrated with light. Just before we left, when we were already in the car, he came and stood a few feet from me. He placed his palms together in the Indian manner and gazed into my eyes at length. I accepted the exchange. We had an intense spiritual communion for some moments. He had felt what I was doing in that place, and since he was thus part of it, there was no reason to hide the plan that he had discovered. In writing these lines I am strongly and vigorously reliving those past moments.

Going back to Trivandrum, my companion, who had observed it all, said to me "It is what I have just seen that reinforces my mystical convictions." Then he added sadly, "I don't have any friends in Paris like the one you just made." I told him that in order to meet someone like the young disciple, one of like mind, you had to come to a place like that. He acknowledged that, and then he added "I think that my mystical search has to take place in France. That's where I have to be." I didn't tell him this, but I thought of the young rich man of the Gospels. At the same time I had the feeling that he was absolutely right. It was back in our country that he would have to make progress on the mystical path. He would have to explore life and gain an intimacy with it in order to acquire, doubtless in another existence, the superhuman strength of absolute detachment.

I could write about many other ashrams in India. I've said that there are thousands of them, and, except for a few, the best known are not the most worthwhile. I think that the biggest lesson you can learn from a long sojourn in India is that we have at home, in the West, exactly that which is necessary for our mystical evolution and the discovery of our inner reality. That is why pilgrimages to ancient sources of knowledge, such as those India has in a thousand ways, are of such great value. They permit you to get to know processes, sometimes thousands of years old, that are offered in consecrated places, to harmonize yourself with them, to extract the essence and project them onto, or rediscover them again, in that which we have near to us in familiar things, so familiar that you don't perceive their importance. To get to know India as my companion and I did is a unique experience. And the reverse is also true. Our guide in Jaipur, in the land of the gurus, asked me to find him a guru, just as we were leaving. He had looked far and wide in that immense country for what he had right in front of him. I hope he finally found one.

In order to finish with the subject of ashrams, I would like to tell you about two others. For the first, I'll do it not because it is more important than others or because it is the best known, but because you will see that it is possible to obtain and perfect in the sincerity of a mystical undertaking and through an absolute confidence in a guru or in a method of spiritual realization. This ashram is that of Sivananda, a guru born in 1887 and who died in 1964. His successor directs the ashram with great authority and consecration. The information we were given put this ashram in Hardwar, but it was wrong. In reality, it is twenty kilometers from there, in Riskikesh. After a quick tour of Hardwar, which is one of the seven holy cities of India, and after looking at some pilgrims and sadhus (even Europeans) in the Ganges, which here was nearly frozen over, we took the road to Rishikesh, paying our chauffeur, a Sikh, and so a kshatrya (a warrior), extra for the additional work.

We arrived at the ashram at twelve fifteen and everything was closed, but we insisted so strongly that a receptionist welcomed us and authorized our visit to the community. At first our chauffeur followed us everywhere. As a good kshatrya, he spoke very loudly and no doubt annoyed all those who were resting or meditating in their cells. We asked him then to wait for us at the car, and we went respectfully about the grounds. No one spoke to us. It was obviously up to us to make contact. A young adept dressed like a monk passed us. Perhaps he was one. I said a few words to him. At first he was hesitant, but he quickly came around. He said that there were some French people at the ashram and asked whether we wanted to meet them. We accepted, naturally, with thanks. He took us to a sort of little house, a kind of separate cell, and called out, and we saw the door open. A woman dressed in white, an ageless woman, came toward us and greeted us in the Indian fashion, her palms together. We presented ourselves and she invited us to go in. We were in a small room painted white, with hardly any furniture, just whatever was necessary for a life of simplicity, even of austerity. At her request we sat on the bed, and she sat on the floor. We spoke for a long, long time, and we learned a great deal about the guru, the ashram, and her own experience. Vibrations of peace and light emanated from that woman, that adept. And yet, what a life of suffering, unhappiness, and crucifixion she had known before she found her way toward spiritual regeneration! And also physical regeneration, for she was stricken with an incurable disease, multiple sclerosis. Quickly understanding that she had become a burden on her family, she succeeded in leaving them, which they wished her to do anyway. Her husband and children had abandoned her when she met the guru and had become his disciple. This was the most painful trial for her, but she overcame it. After seven years in the ashram she was then cured! And there in front of us, as she told her story, she was the image of the most absolute serenity. She was the instrument, the vehicle, the support of the divine life expressing itself on the physical plane. When we were readying to leave, feeling and seeing everything that manifested through her, I knelt before her and asked humbly for her blessing. She drew back, brought her hands together, saying in a voice that was almost fearful "No! Oh! No! Only the guru can do that." But I insisted, and she finally murmured "Yes, but only mentally." And I can affirm that through her the blessing from On High came over me, powerful and bursting with light. It is unfortunate, my dear companion, that you didn't follow my example. I understood the discomfort that you showed, but, believe me, there was a lot to learn from this intermediary that came from much higher than her. All the conditions had been created to that end, and at that point she was the instrument and vehicle of the On High for a few moments of profound receptivity! Just before we left her, she gave us a little book written in English that she had published privately: the story of her life, of her spiritual ascension under the guidance of her guru. She assured me that she would inform him of our encounter. She was a sort of prelude on the mystical plane. Yvonne Lebeau, we will never forget you!

At the entrance to the ashram of Sivananda, there is an obelisk on which are written some enlightening words. Since I think that they will be very meaningful to you, I will translate them here:

OM
The essential doctrines of the principal religions of the world.

Know yourself and be free.
Hinduism

The kingdom of Heaven is within you.
Christianity

There Is No other God but Allah.
Islam

For the whole world here is the law: Everything is transitory.
Buddhism

Never do evil; in truth, that is the only religion.
Jainism

Purity of thought, word, and action; the essence of religion.
Zoroastrianism

I am the One who Is.
Judaism

Blame yourself as you blame others.
Forgive others as you forgive yourself.
Confucius

There is only one God and his name is Truth.
The guru is wonderful.
Sikhism

I am that which is real.
Suffism

Hear no evil, see no evil, speak no evil.
Shintoism

All religions are one, and they teach a divine life. Love the whole world. Serve the whole world. Practice Ahimsa (non-violence), Satya (Truth), and Brachmacharya (Continence). Be an altruist. Seek for the immortal, divine life.
The Heart of Religion

God is love, the only religion is the religion of love, or of the heart. Feel for others what you feel for yourselves. This religion will give the world peace and happiness.
Sivananda

Seek
Find
Enter
Rest in God
OM
Universal Prayer

Oh, adorable land of mercy and love,
We salute you. We prostrate ourselves before You.
You are Sachidananda.
You are omnipresent,
Omnipresent and omniscient.
You are beyond all others.

Give us an understanding heart,
Clear vision, and a stable mind,
Faith, devotion, and wisdom.
Give us interior, spiritual strength
To resist temptations and control our minds.
Free us from egotism, envy and hate.
Fill our hearts with divine virtue.
Let us recognize You in all Your names and forms
Let us never forget You,

Let us always sing Your glory.
Let Your Name be always on our lips.

Let us live in You forever.

This prayer is not at all sectarian in any way. It can be used in course of any religious meetings. It is cosmopolitan and it all faiths. It is a beautiful universal prayer, and you can repeat it every day at home, as well as at public occasions. It will unite the whole world, spiritualize your activities, and reveal the golden secret of the divine life.
Swami Sivananda

Be good and full of compassion.

OM
Twenty rules

1. Get up at 4:00 a.m., and practice japa[1] and meditation.
2. Sit in the postures called padma or sidda,[2] For the japa and the dhyana.[3]
3. Take sattvic[4] food. Don't overload your stomach.
4. Practice charity in giving one-tenth of your revenue, that is, one anna for each rupee.[5]
5. Every day, study one chapter of the Bhagavad-Gita.
6. Preserve virya.[6] Sleep alone.
7. Do not smoke narcotics, Or drink intoxicating beverages, Or eat like a king.

---

[1] Japa is the repetition of a mantra, a sacred word, or a prayer.
[2] Padma and sidda are asanas, or yoga postures.
[3] Dhyana is meditation.
[4] Sattvic means spiritual.
[5] The anna in India is one-tenth of a rupee.
[6] Virya is the life force.

8. Fast on ekasadi[7] days. Or eat fruit and drink only milk.
9. Observe mouna[8] two hours a day and during meals.
10. Tell the truth, no matter what. Speak in a soft voice.
11. Eliminate your needs, lead a happy and satisfying life.
12. Don't hurt anyone's feelings. Be good to the world.
13. Think of the mistakes you have made. Look to your conscience.
14. Don't count on Servants. Rely on yourself.
15. Think about God when you get up and when you go to bed.
16. Always wear a japa-mala[9] around your neck or in your pocket.
17. Your motto: Simple life, elevated thoughts.
18. Serve the Sadhus, the Sanyasins,[10] the poor, the sick, and those who suffer.
19. Have a room reserved for meditation. Lock it firmly.
20. Keep a daily spiritual journal. And keep to your consecrated life.

These twenty rules include the spiritual essence of yoga and vedanta. Follow them strictly. Don't be self-indulgent. You will achieve the supreme happiness.

Swami Sivananda

> Be good.
> Do what is right.

You must have noticed that each of these texts began with the sacred syllable OM. I will take this occasion to explain that OM and AUM are identical. OM includes AUM. In Sanskrit, O is considered to be a diphthong that combines A and U. OM, according to the sacred authorities, is a single phoneme (advaita), nonetheless formed of three elements. Another simpler way of

---

[7] Spiritual days.
[8] Mouna means silence.
[9] Japa is a Hindu rosary.
[10] Sanyasin is one who is engaged in renouncing life (sanyasa).

saying this is that A and U melded together to give the sound O in phonetic Sanskrit. OM is a liturgical exclamation, something that people say before and after the recitation of every sacred text, no matter how short it is, a simple blessing, for example. So priests, gurus, and the simple faithful often pronounce the celebrated OM. According to one of our guides, OM is never pronounced alone. It begins and ends a prayer. But I don't agree with this simple explanation. OM in itself has a great vibratory value.

The second and last ashram that I want to speak about is that of Sri Aurobindo. Since it is very well known because of the many works written about it, notably those of Satprem, and because the teachings of that ashram can be found in Sri Aurobindo's books, I will have very little to say about it. It was on the 26th of October that we went to Pondicherry. The trip from Madras, one hundred and seventy kilometers, took us three hours. It was raining torrents that day. The monsoon there was endless, and there were many floods. According to what we learned in Madras, there was a dangerous rivalry between the ashram and Auroville, which all of you have certainly heard about. This rivalry was causing terrible friction, but that doesn't concern us.

I am particularly interested in it because from the age of eighteen and for long years afterwards Sri Aurobindo was my Master of thinking. Furthermore, a dozen years before, the Mother, Sri Aurobindo's companion, had sent me his photograph, and some rose petals in an envelope on which she had written in her own hand *For Raymond Bernard.* Such delicate attention on her part, when I knew she was so busy, moved me profoundly. Another much more recent event made me want to visit that ashram. The day after the end of the world-wide Convention in Paris, someone had tried to find me at the Hotel Concorde-La Fayette and finally had left a message asking me to telephone a certain number that I knew to be that of the Hotel Meridien, which was near where I was staying. And so it was that, having called as he wished, I had a conversation with Mister

Navajata who told me he was the president of Auroville and, if memory serves, the manager of the Sri Aurobindo ashram. Having gone to Paris to attend a session of UNESCO, he wanted to participate in the part of our world-wide Convention authorized for non-members. I told him that it was over, but I informed him that I was going to India again. He told me that in these perilous times there must be strong ties among the ancient, serious, and authentic spiritual movements. I could only agree with him. I was to see him in India, if we should both be there at the same time. In any case, he was supposed to leave the necessary instructions.

The city of Pondicherry in India is like others, but it is dominated by the ashram of Sri Aurobindo. The ashram possesses numerous buildings and factories and provides work for around two thousand people, many of whom, especially foreigners, are unpaid. We went to the administrative office of the ashram. Mister Navajata was away in Delhi, but we were warmly welcomed by his son who spoke French very well. For once we were able to have a long conversation in our own language, instead of in English. Our host answered our questions with a frank openness, not trying to hide the disagreement between the ashram and Auroville. He was perfectly confident that the right was on Mister Navajata's side and the problems were only temporary, being provoked by an insignificant group. I listened to what he was explaining to us without saying a word. In any community of human beings it is inevitable that problems will sometimes arise, generally caused by some irresponsible person. The right, however, which comes from On High, and not from humankind, always triumphs.

Then we went shopping in a few of the many stores that the ashram operates, finding diverse and unexpected articles to buy. Afterwards we went to visit the home of Sri Aurobindo and Mother. It is open every day for only five minutes at the end of the morning. Walking around the grounds and entering the rooms where they both lived and where Sri Aurobindo and

Mother meditated for so many years, I was startled by an intense interior feeling. As a matter of fact, I was in the place where I had been so often in my thoughts. The spiritual vibrations of the Presence were nearly tangible. We left filled with that unique ambience, and from afar, the crowd being very great, we saluted the marble tomb covered with flowers where incense was burning, the tomb of Sri Aurobindo and Mother.

It was lunch time. Our guide took us to one of the ashram's restaurants, and we both thought that Mister Navajata would not have sent us there, for his son had told us "You'll hear a lot of things, both good and bad. You draw your own conclusions." In that restaurant we did hear quite a bit while we ate. A young American of eighteen years who had been in the ashram for nine years, explained to us, in excellent French, the reproaches made against Mister Navajata. According to that young man, Mother had said that she didn't want him to manage the ashram after her death, and all the frictions and differences turned around that. To his enemies, Mister Navajata was an imposter who had taken over for himself. But the question you can't help asking when you hear such a proposition, on the one hand, is since the ashram has an administrative committee, and it appointed Mister Navajata, no one has the right to deny it, and on the other hand, the ashram couldn't run itself. I think that that regrettable situation will sort itself out. The malcontents will leave and everything will get back to normal. We could have foreseen that Mother's death would provoke problems because she had a powerful personality, and her departure left a big void. But the problems will be solved and the void filled.

Immediately after our lunch we left for Auroville. I don't know whether the guide showed us the whole place, but for me it was an immense disillusionment. The city that we expected to see wasn't there. Only one building, the Matrimandir, which was supposed to be the center of the consecrated city, had been started, and apart from it there was no other building, nothing, just fields as far as you could see, most of which, according to our guides, didn't belong to Auroville or to the ashram. People who come here hoping to see the promised development must be very disappointed. Many people think that construction of the city been completed.

My companion and I were rather eager to leave that place. All that we saw and heard and which disappointed us can take nothing away from the value of the work inspired by Sri Aurobindo and Mother's accomplishments. It is their home, moreover, that we always remember with emotion and veneration. And I can't help remembering what our guide in Trivandrum said "Once the guru is gone..." That's where the whole difference between an ashram and a Traditional Order resides. In the latter, the transmission of knowledge takes place over centuries, and the torch is passed from hand to hand. In an ashram, it is first of all the memory of the guru that is perpetuated. This does not mean, in any way, that an ashram doesn't have spiritual value. An ashram has a permanent one—the teachings of the departed guru. But as time goes by and the new spiritual needs of generations grow, even if it is only sufficient to adjust knowledge to more advanced times and circumstances, there must be a revolution in the preservation of teachings, in training, and also in techniques followed. That is possible and has always been accomplished in an ancient, authentic, traditional Order. Is that possible in an ashram where for a definite period of time a particular teaching was applied? That is the whole question.

In any case, if I thought it was worthwhile to describe the above circumstances to you, it was because it was my duty to do it. You would have learned about the situation sooner or later anyway. When that happens, you will already have learned about it in the pages of this *Letter from Nowhere,* and you will know how to keep your own end up and do your part. In this regard, you must never judge, but know, and this knowing is understanding. Always treat all evidence of truth with respect, wherever it is found and however it is expressed. The truth is forever one, and the paths that lead to it are always diverse. The innumerable ashrams of India are a fundamental element of the religious life of a religious people. There is no way they could not exist in that country so avid for wisdom, knowledge, and spirituality. All the ashrams are respectable and even venerated. But I doubt whether they can do very much for a Westerner these days. At best they might give him whatever is already at the disposition of any seeker in our countries. Everything that India can offer in the way of knowledge, of training, or of techniques, the West already has under other names and different symbols, but that does not mean that India has nothing for the West. It has its Holy Writings that go back thousands of years, and its authentic, ancient techniques that were long ago transmitted to the West. However, the greatest thing India can give to the West is its profoundly religious, mystical and tolerant spirit, of which I have spoken at length.

Finally, the Hindu searches for a teacher who he feels has knowledge to give him, and he is not tricked or dominated by appearances. His guru, his instructor, his master is not separated into two beings or parties—one being wisdom and the other a human being. The Hindu who chooses a guru recognizes in all his master's words and gestures a lesson he must welcome and the presence of the divine—and this includes what we with our restricted, Western mentality would judge to be incompatible with a state of wisdom. That is sometimes difficult for us to understand, but isn't that the most evident mark of veneration and love?

In an earlier *Letter from Nowhere*, I suggested some books that can enlighten you, if Hindu wisdom interests you. One among them, if read attentively and slowly—because, at the beginning, it can appear to be difficult—is a spiritual enchantment. It's a book of nearly seven hundred pages entitled *Hinduism, Texts and Sacred Traditions*, by Anne-Marie Esnoul. You can get it from Rosicrucian Editions. I personally found a source of inspiration and meditation in this book.

In the next *Letter from Nowhere*, I'll tell you about some interesting encounters, and I'll cover the subject of Tibetan

Buddhism, in the light of my encounter with venerable Lamas in Daramsala and in Gangtok, in Sikkim. I trust that these subjects will interest you.

                Very sincerely yours,
                Raymond Bernard

7

JULY 1978

Grand Lamas of Tibet

Dear Friends,

All year long I have resolutely discussed India in every *Letter from Nowhere*. I have told you about the trip my companion and I took. Evidently it would take a whole book to relate all the experiences we encountered and the discoveries we made on our pilgrimage to the sources over a forty-five day period. But my purpose is especially to provide you with some fundamental points of reference that will make it possible for you, if you go to India, to see beyond the obvious and avoid being caught in the snares of illusion. My purpose is to urge you not to be content with only being a tourist in places of immemorial wisdom. It would be better to save your time, your fatigue, and, naturally, your money. My companion and I saw organized tours of only eight days' duration! What could these people see and understand in so little time? As for us, sleeping only a few hours every night, it took a month and a half to gather as much as possible, while neglecting, most of the time, the purely touristic aspects of that immense country and its incomparable diversity.

In this last *Letter from Nowhere* to be dedicated to the subject of India, I'll tell you openly and frankly about some of the problems we ran into from the point of view of the organization of our trip, so that you can know in advance about some deceiving commercial practices that will catch you, if you don't know about them, and about which there is nothing you can do, over there, once they get you. I'll tell you what to avoid, and about the attitude to adopt in certain circumstances. If we had been only simple tourists, at several junctures during our trip we probably would have given up and gone home. But we had gone there to look for something infinitely superior to tourism, and if we found what we were looking for, it is not thanks to the agencies, by and large, that we dealt with. It was our own efforts, and certainly the help of the On High, that enabled us to attain the ends we were looking for.

In this same *Letter from Nowhere,* the last of the India series, I'll extract from my journal the daily, chronological facts. You will have a digest of what I told you in the preceding letters, and additional observations and explanations about the organization of our trip and the problems we had to solve. I think that with this information you will be able to avoid, in large part, any difficulties, and I'll be happy to be the one who has informed you about them in advance. But we haven't come to these final matters yet. First we have to look at the pilgrimage that we have undertaken together through the *Letter from Nowhere* every four months. Let us then return to India in quest of more knowledge and light.

In my last letter I spoke about ashrams, and you know that they are essentially communities gathered around a guru or perpetuating his memory. In point of fact, we could say that in the West, the mystical and traditional Orders are ashrams, with the basic difference that the purpose of these communities is to perpetuate, in constant evolution, a teaching that has to be adapted to new times and circumstances. Outwardly, this teaching remains impersonal and it doesn't imply devotion, or worship, of a living Master, nor a teacher who may be deceased. That's the basic difference, and it's an important one. This aside, the similarities are remarkable, especially in regard to the practical problems that we encounter, including those on the material plane. But the ways that Indians understand the problems of material substance are quite peculiar. India inherited a past that has gone on for thousands of years, and the society is founded on the notion of offering, gift, or sacrifice. So there is nothing shocking for the Indian to see that every ashram has many boutiques and stores where things are sold. The idea of shameful commercialism is non-existent there, among Hindus and non-believers. Moreover, in all the temples and at the foot of every statue, the Indians toss money, with love and respect. In all of that there is no idolatry or fetishism. The gift or offering symbolizes an intention, or is a simple sacrifice. Neither I nor my companion was put off by it. After all, in a certain way, we do the same thing in quite similar circumstances. Some people say that is superstition, forgetting the power of intention, and if they really think about it, they see that there is nothing superstitious in that act. In the temples of India, there are piles of coins meant for good works every day. I'm sure that all that money goes for its intended purpose.

About forty kilometers from Cochin, in the state of Kerala, you can find the ashram of Shankaracharya. The site is splendid and the buildings are graceful. There are only Brahmans there who have a very pronounced sense of caste. An old man explained the life of Shankara to us. By contrast, when we got to one of the little sanctuaries sheltered by the main building, a Brahman and his helper held a special puja (ceremony) for us in honor of Sarasvati, the goddess of wisdom. Our rupees were received, as it were, at a distance. We put the rupees in front of us, before the altar. It was the same for the tip we gave to the Brahman who took us to meet the managers of the ashram. To receive this offering, he put his hands together, forming a cup beneath our hands, and he caught the money that we dropped to him. For him, as for all Brahmans, my friend and I were untouchables. In spite of all that, we both really loved this place where Bhakti Yoga—the Way of Devotion—is practiced.

Others received our offerings with fewer problems, and we were the ones to be reserved, simply leaving the money on the nearest furniture. That's what happened on Friday, the 14th of October in Nepal where the Guru Vidya Bhushan agreed to accept us as chelas, that is, as disciples. I must tell you about this experience, because it is interesting. We arrived the night before in Katmandu, and as soon as possible we explained to our guide the real reason for our visit. He wanted to please us, and having asked his own guru, the latter acquiesced immediately. We came to a desolate street and, in front of a low house the guide told us to wait. From the door that the guide opened for us we could see a barely furnished room, and in front of us, on a large divan, the guru sat, his legs folded in the lotus position. In front of him were two women who seemed to be consulting him. He was holding one of their hands in his. Seeing us, he told them to leave, and I understand that he told them to come back later. They went away and the guru received us with a great deal of amiability. He asked us to sit down on the big sofa. I sat down between him and my companion. We were both in the tailor position, which is very similar to the lotus position. Our young guide, in order to serve as our interpreter, sat down in front of us on the floor next to the guru. And again I told the story of what we were looking for. While speaking and waiting for the translation, I looked around the room. On the walls there were some prints of gods and goddesses, and in front of us was a big picture of our guru's teacher. As for our guru himself, he was dressed in white, but his clothes were not very clean. His brown, sort of sandy hair, was long, and his eyes were clear. He was skinny, nervous, and I don't know why, but in certain of his attitudes he bothered me. Mentally, I beg him to forgive me for this impression that I haven't really looked into. Like my companion, I was eager to hear with respect and devotion whatever he could tell us. To his question as to whether we had personal gurus, we answered negatively. Finally, he said "What do you want to know?" We asked him to speak about meditation. He did so at length, about an hour, taking the translation into account. His message was easy to understand and I will give it to you now.

At first the guru established a parallelism that seemed to be very important to him:

Head	Brahma	Heaven
Heart	Vishnu	Earth
Navel	Shiva	Hell

It was on this parallelism that it was first necessary to meditate, and then he added several refinements that I can mention here. Moreover, it is clear that this first impression is a sufficient base for meditation, especially when we remember that in the Hindu Trimurti Brahma represents the creator, Vishnu the conserver (who maintains things), and Shiva the destroyer. Now reflect a few moments with me. Man, being a microcosm, reflects the macrocosm. He is all in All. But also he has All in him. He is the universe in miniature, and if he really knows himself, it is the universe and the gods that he knows. Thus we understand the power of *Know Thyself* engraved on the pediment of the temple at Delphi. Furthermore, it is the individual himself who decides whether to direct his life from the head, the heart, or the navel, that is to say, with the creative power of heaven, the calm, balanced certitude of the heart, or the torments and destruction of hell. Meditate on these first ideas given by the guru, as I have just done for you. You can go very far in your conclusions and the insight gained. You will understand that your happiness or unhappiness depends on you, and not on anyone else. It all depends on the level where you choose to place yourself.

After having established the first parallelism without making any comment, the Guru Vidya Bhushan continued with another enumeration that I will let you think about, but this time without any explanation. This list has to do with the bonds that exist between the fingers of the hand and different parts of the body, as follows:

> Thumb: Venus, connected with the skull.
> Index: Jupiter, connected with the eye and the ear.
> Middle finger: Saturn, connected with the nose and the throat.
> Ring finger: Sun, connected with the heart.
> Little finger: Mercury, connected with the navel.

These bits of information must be perfectly understood and remembered in order to produce the kind of meditation recommended by the guru. In the practice of this kind of meditation, you are required to assume a definite position and to adopt a breathing exercise before you meditate. I have mentioned the lotus position on several occasions, and it is well known. I think it is hard for a Westerner to assume, and it is harder still to stay in the lotus position unless you practice it for a long time. Therefore, I believe another position will do just as well: feet flat on the floor, hands on the knees, the back perfectly straight. Holding this position, you must give yourself up to an internal exercise of rhythmic breathing. A book about this exercise, entitled *Hara: The Vital Center of Man* by Karlfried Graf Durckheim, appeared a few years ago.

In this exercise, the tip of the thumb of each hand must be placed at the base of the little finger of the same hand, and both hands are turned upwards. The whole chest, I repeat, must be held upright. The teeth should be together, the lips slightly open, and the eyes closed. Breathing must, in a manner of speaking, be turned inwards. It must be rhythmically normal and not jerky, coming not from the lungs, but from the abdomen. It must be done slowly, very slowly. If you have the time, you should take twenty-one deep breaths. Let me remind you that this exercise takes place before the meditation.

Concerning the meditation itself, Guru Vidya Bhushan's teaching is as follows: a person is a complex made up of the union of a body, a life, and a soul. In this complex, as regards the material world, the body and the soul rest, but the life itself never rests. Actually, if there were no life in the human complex, dreaming would be impossible, for the body would be dead and the soul would be solely in the higher spheres. Life attaches itself to the soul in order to leave the body and dissolve in the universe. The purpose of meditation is to permit the life to rest too. What should the subject of meditation be? It must not be made up of mental or other images, for, in that case, the life will not rest. Furthermore, for the same reason, thoughts won't do either. But it is evident that in the beginning it is difficult if not impossible not to have images or thoughts in the mind. You can get over this difficulty by mentally looking at a figure and slowly letting it disappear. Meditation must be done in a calm atmosphere to avoid any distraction. And finally you have to forget your body too. Nothing must remain—an emptiness as absolute as possible must be attained.

You must then concentrate between your eyes and make a ray or beam leave you, descend the rim of your nose and stop twenty centimeters in front of you. The guru repeats "No further!" explaining that to do so would separate us from the world. It is when this experimental stage has been reached that you can remember your previous incarnations and see God. The best times to meditate are at four o'clock in the morning and in the evening. As for how long to meditate, you must decide in advance and the meditation will stop by itself. This is the meditation practice recommended by this particular guru. I've told you about it for your information, for we were not forbidden from sharing it.

In the explanations of this guru, what is particularly interesting is the information about the relationship between the fingers and parts of the body. We questioned him further about this matter, and he told us what we expected, that this knowledge can be used to improve the physical state of the body. In this case, it is the thumb that becomes the center of the treatment. Suppose you want to improve your eyes. You should place the tip of your index finger on the base of your thumb, with both hands, and go on with deep breaths and silent, peaceful meditation. If the improvement concerns the nose or throat, use the tips of your middle fingers, and so forth.

That meeting with the Guru Vidya Bhushan from Katmandu, in Nepal, was very interesting for us. Just before we left him, he gave each of us a personal mantra. He allowed us to take his photograph and we separated in mutual harmony, peace, and satisfaction at having met. That was the same guru who told me, taking my hand in his own, that I would leave the physical plane at the age of eighty-nine years, and doing the same with my companion, he predicted that he would depart at the age of eighty-six. My companion and I are looking forward to growing so old.

In the description of our trip I come now to a part that was one of the most interesting, if not the most interesting: our contacts with the Tibetan refugees in India. We infinitely regret China's invasion of Tibet and we sympathize, with all our being, with the sad situation of the refugees in a strange world, of those who chose exile rather than live in their own country under the domination of a powerful neighbor. But at the same time we can ask whether the events that came to pass in that part of the world were not cosmically desired. As a matter of fact, Tibet was a secret territory possessing an incontestable mystical knowledge, but it was turned inwards on itself and forbade any approach by seekers from other countries. Without the Chinese invasion, it is quite probable that that territory would still be forbidden and the world would not be able to benefit from Tibetan Wisdom, and Tibet would have remained, as often has been the case in the past, the country where authors and false explorers would go to find their message or strange adventure. They could put forth any thesis or tell any story, and no one could check up on them.

Furthermore, the new era has begun. The truth must be spread widely. The light must no longer be hidden under a bushel, and it is also a fact that we have an urgent need to fill the vacuum created by the ailing major religions.

Contrary to the traditional and mystical Orders, what Tibet has brought us out of its territory, by force of circumstances, is not mystical and esoteric knowledge and techniques, but a religious science. Concerning the mystical and esoteric knowledge and techniques, they were already known among Western circles of initiates and traditional Orders, which in several ways and particularly by contacts and legations had received the transmission of the secret Tibetan Wisdom and had included it in their teachings, adapting it to their own terminology. This is why those who have been able to have access to the most authentic Tibetan sources now available in the West, and who have advanced far enough in their traditional studies, have all agreed that what they have learned they had already known in different words. This explains why I had so much inner satisfaction and elation to meet Tibetans and talk to them about the Western tradition. They immediately felt a moving sympathy for me and my companion. As for the grand Lamas that we made contact with, they knew beyond all words. However, we did get a big surprise in Daramsala. Tsering, our dear Tibetan guide, had taken us to the young French woman whose address had been given me by Gaby Genevet, and we were walking around in the Tibetan village. I was thinking of the world-wide Convention that was held in Paris in August when the young French woman turned to Tsering and said to him: "but that's the convention that you heard about on the radio and that you told us about." At the other end of the world, the Tibetan who had welcomed us in the surprising circumstances that I will relate, had paid close attention to short-wave news mentioning the World-wide Convention of a Western Order! Isn't that one more proof, and we have received so many, that from a higher sphere someone was watching after us on every step of our trip.

Here is how we got to know Tsering. We arrived in Daramsala on the 20th of October in the evening from Jammu, with a Sikh guide who was especially interesting and amusing. Five hours on the road brought us near to the Himalayas, and we were now in the cool air amid splendid mountain scenery, after having spent days in heavy heat. On the morning of the 3rd of October, at eight-thirty we left for the Tibetan village just ten kilometers from Daramsala, in the mountains. Wanting to pursue our research alone, at the risk of compromising it, but being very careful, we sent the car and the guide away, to come back in the evening at seven o'clock. We were alone. Wanting to know the location of the hotel where Nicole lived, whose address had been given us by Gaby Genevet, we happened upon a cafe full of young Europeans, Canadians, etc., and we were immediately followed by a smiling twenty-seven year old Tibetan who instantly understood our purpose. We thought that his purpose in guiding us was to earn a few rupees, but we learned later how wrong we were, because we had with us an envoy from Heaven, Tsering.

First of all he took us to the hotel that we were looking for, because, not only did he know that hotel, but he knew Nicole, the French woman we were looking for. And we quickly learned of the esteem and affection that she was held in everyone in the Tibetan village. Nicole stayed with us a long time until she was called away to participate in a special ceremony, but she came back in the evening. Since Tsering had no other special obligation, he stayed with us until our departure and thanks to him we were able to learn a great deal. Actually, without him, our visit to Daramsala would have been a failure. But permit me to doubt that such a turn of events could ever have happened.

I would like at this point to come back to the exile of the Tibetans, about whom I have already given my opinion. Their fate had already been cosmically determined because of the coming of the new age, but that does not at all mean that in exile the Tibetans will not one day return to their homeland, to a country having regained its full independence. Certainly this eventuality won't take place soon. However, I have an inescapable feeling that divine justice will be accomplished, and it is possible that China herself will one day make this historic decision. An opinion that is shared by a large number of savants and seekers is that while waiting for freedom, the exiles who are erudite or devoted to a higher calling, whatever their level of understanding, are the only way to bring about a large diffusion, in all countries, of Tibetan religious thought. In order to convince yourself of this, just consider the impressive number of Tibetan communities now living in Western countries. The most decisive opinion seems to me to be that of Lama Anagarika Govinda, whose culture and training in every way are essentially Tibetan, even though he is not one himself. His book *The Land of White Clouds* was recommended by Rosicrucian Editions, and appreciated by everyone who read it. Now there is another book, *The Fundamentals of Tibetan Mysticism*. It is a little more difficult, but very important. Rosicrucian Editions won't hesitate to recommend it, if they haven't already. And in the Preface of this book, Lama Anagarika Govinda writes:

> "Because of Tibet's natural isolation and its inaccessibility (made more extreme by the political conditions of the last few centuries), it has been able to preserve the most ancient traditions, which are not only pure but still alive.
> "They are the knowledge of the power hidden in the human soul, and the highest esoteric teachings of the Indian sages. But given the disruptive forces that are turning the world upside down, which did not spare the Tibetan people, and tore Tibet from its isolation, all of these spiritual conquests must either disappear or become the salvation, in the future, of a higher human culture. Tomo Geche Rimpoche, recognized as one of the great spiritual authorities of modern Tibet, a true master of interior vision, saw all of this coming and so left his mountain hermitage secluded from the world where for

twelve years he had been meditating, and proclaimed that the time had come to give to the rest of the world the spiritual treasures that Tibet had been safeguarding for more than a thousand years, because humankind is at a crossroads of grave decisions. Before us is the way leading to power through the mastery of natural forces—a way of slavery and self-destruction—or that of Illumination, the Bottisattva-marga, which by the mastery of the inner power leads to Freedom and Self-realization."

The situation could not be treated more clearly and precisely. It is also a testimony in our time for that which the Tradition can repeat only with its sacred work and incomparable activities.

But let us return to Daramsala and find our friend Tsering. We went with him into that part of the city that the Indians call Upper Daramsala. Maybe it is to differentiate the Indian village that is located much further down the mountain. The Tibetan village covers a large area but is not imposing. However, since the streets are very narrow, and the people spend most of each day outdoors, it seems more crowded than it actually is. In the middle of the village there are big prayer mills, that are lined up side by side on a kind of promontory leading to the two main streets, and a few meters away is a special building painted in bright colors. A much bigger prayer mill that one walks around from left to right to make it turn. My companion and I did that once. We made the smaller prayer-mills turn several times one way or the other to face one or the other of the main streets.

It doesn't take long to visit the village. We stopped for some time in front of one house because we saw that it was the house of a famous Tibetan medical doctor who was known to have special knowledge, like many of his truly initiated colleagues. That man was the personal doctor to the Dalai Lama, who lived in Daramsala at that time. A few minutes later we went back and entered the doctor's house. Actually, my companion didn't feel well. He thought that he was suffering from the beginning of jaundice, and if that was true, it would interrupt our trip and cause me no end of grief. In the doctor's office there were a lot of people, Tibetans, Indians, naturally, and many Westerners. We had to have an interpreter with us because the doctor didn't speak English very well, and not even a little bit of French. Happily, we had Tsering with us. The room we waited in was a veritable drugstore. A whole wall was covered with shelves filled with containers full of strange pills of all sorts the size of marbles. Two medical assistants seated at a table read the prescriptions that the doctor had just sent out and put the medicine in dark, little paper sacks. Thanks to Tsering we were quickly shown into the consultation room. The doctor was, of course, a Lama. Tsering and another young Tibetan interpreted what he had to say. In our brief conversation I told the doctor what we were doing and why. In regard to our Traditions, Tsering was very forceful in convincing the doctor who we were.

As for the consultation, the doctor took the patient's pulse, wrapping his fingers around his upper arms. His eyes were half-closed, and he seemed to be in a state of extreme concentration. For my companion, there was a quick diagnosis. The doctor knew what was wrong. For five days, three times a day, my companion took, before and after his meals, some pills that we bought in the next room. He chewed them up and swallowed them with warm water. I then asked the Tibetan doctor to examine me. He listened to my pulse, and as if he were in a trance, he felt along my arms, unbuttoned my shirt and pushed on certain parts of my left breast. I could feel that those parts were painful. The doctor spoke and my interpreter immediately gave the English translation: "Blood, heart". It would be long. For months I would have to take pills that he prescribed in Tibetan writing through his assistants. I asked him for a two-month long prescription, but then I decided to wait until my return to France, thinking that all I had learned in India was much more important than my little physical self.

Since my companion had to take his pills for only five days, he did so, with his glass of warm water. He kept complaining about how bad they tasted. After five days he was perfectly well. For my part, unfortunately I forgot about the pills that the Tibetan doctor had prescribed. When I got back to France I was very occupied with many activities. I remembered them on the 7th of December in the evening, and I decided to take them the next day. But it was too late. My myocardial infarction was upon me. In the last *Letter from Nowhere* I declared that in our lives, certain events, experiences, or maladies are, in effect, programmed, and we have to put up with them in order to learn more. Concerning my heart attack, I have already told you about my reaction to it. My encounter with the Tibetan doctor, the pills he prescribed for my condition, and what later occurred are further examples. I must tell you here that the pills the Tibetan doctor prescribed are not made of chemical elements. They are a secret compound of the Tibetan doctor which he prepares himself.

After we visited the Tibetan doctor, Tsreing took us into a temple. It was outside the village, about a kilometer away. There were many houses around it, some big ones that were monasteries, and many smaller ones where important Lamas resided. That was where the Dalai Lama's house was. In other words, it was the religious village of the Tibetans of Daramsala, a tiny Lhassa where the modest residence of the Dalai Lama symbolized the immense deserted Potala, the whole thing being just a model of what the Tibetans want to recreate in their country in the future, because no Tibetan can believe that the exile they are suffering is final. And I can still hear Tsering's answer to my question about what in Tibet, the "roof of the world," could interest a great power: "It is what is in the soil, in wealth and minerals." And his smile hid a few tears when he added, "For us Tibetans, the greatest, incomparable wealth is in verdant nature, in flowers, and in healing plants."

The Tibetan temple of Daramsala is very important for what it represents, along with the fact that the Dalai Lama is a refugee in that part of India. It is not imposing because of its size, but because of what it symbolizes—the religious heart of the Tibetans in exile, just as St. Peter's in Rome is the heart of the Vatican and so of Catholicism. Naturally my companion and I meditated at length in that temple, and we respectfully looked at the poor religious treasures that the Dalai Lama was able to bring with him during his flight into exile. There they have taken on inestimable value for the Tibetans. It was in that temple while the smiling Tsering was showing us some admirable religious objects that, by chance, he told us "I made this!" and I immediately perceived the intense mysticism of that young Tibetan whose words were impregnated with exceptional wisdom. It would take a whole *Letter from Nowhere* for me to tell you what he shared with us.

Gaby Genevet had recommended us to an important Lama, so Nicole and Tsering took us to see him. Even though he speaks no other language than Tibetan, his great wisdom was such that he was invited to go to the United States to participate in an important colloquium, and he had been received with utmost respect. With Tsering translating, we had a long conversation about important subjects with him, and with an immense gentleness he invited us to have dinner with him that evening. Since we were to leave the Tibetan village at seven o'clock we agreed to meet at his house at five o'clock, but before we parted, even though we were to see him soon, he wanted to give us his blessing. A little later Tsering suggested that he drive us to meet his Lama who had instructed him and filled the role of guru for him. Of course we immediately accepted. Tsering's Lama lived in the monastery, and since Tsering was with us we had no problem getting in. The Lama's little cell was at the end of a long corridor. At the mention of his name, Tsering was given permission to enter and for us to follow. How the place radiated purity, power, and saintliness! I took the seat which was offered in front of the

Lama, who himself was seated in the lotus position in a sort of closed stall. Before him was a Tibetan manuscript that he was reading when we arrived. My companion was on my left facing the Lama too. Tsering sat very close to be able to translate, and Nicole, who had given us so much help, was there also.

By all evidence we were in the presence of a great and holy Lama. He was eighty-seven years old, Tsering told us, and day and night he was in prayer seated in the same place, but from time to time, he added laughing, he had to get out and restore the circulation in his legs like a young man. I felt and saw that that holy Lama had developed great abilities, even though like every true Sage he hid them and didn't flaunt them. He was one of the closest spiritual counsellors to the Dalai Lama, his director of consciousness, if you will. There was, properly speaking, no conversation with him. Words were useless. He quickly looked at us, and we could feel the power in his eyes. That was sufficient to transmit, and for us it was sufficient to receive, and much was transmitted and received. At the moment we were to leave, as a sign of benediction and transfer of spiritual energy, according to the custom of Sages and even of simple Tibetans, he took a white scarf and put it around my neck. Drawing me toward him he held my forehead against his for a long moment. Then he did the same with my companion, and I hope that for him, as for me, that was the grand experience when a fierce but calming flash full of unformulated knowledge which would take shape later and shoots forth out of the consciousness of the one who is able to receive. shot into the depths of my consciousness. I knew how to receive that knowledge. It would take some shape and be sorted out later.

Tsering was ecstatic. We had met his Lama, and his Lama had welcomed and accepted us. We went back to the village that I would describe as profane, even though every Tibetan is more or less religious, and Tsering asked us to visit his home. We accepted gratefully. Oh, Tsering, my young and holy Tibetan friend, what a fine example you would make for so many of people! Imagine, my dear friends, a modest room, but big enough, divided into two equal parts in the center of which was a window permitting you to see from one side to the other. This other part was Tsering's marvelous sacred sanctuary, his chapel for meditations and experience—a chapel always illuminated. And from the part where he lived, fashioning little metallic pieces of art that he sold to a merchant and so earned a living, Tsering could always see his chapel! My feelings were very elevated in Tsering's home, during the short time we stayed there, and our meditation in the sanctuary will always remain in my memory. When we left his home, he too gave us his blessing with a white scarf, and I can tell you that I received it with profound humility. The divine essence is in each of us, manifesting itself in our inner being, and it did so through us in a moving communion.

At five o'clock we went back to the home of the benevolent Lama who had invited us. The meal was typically Tibetan: Mo-mo, a kind of pasta surrounded by meat, tea with salted butter, and a very special Tibetan bread that was excellent. In the course of the meal, the Lama tried to weave the thread that my companion and I could use to count the beads of our Tibetans rosary. It was a great honor and the indication that the Lama accepted us in his powerful spiritual sphere. Every moment of a holy repast is unforgettable, and towards six-thirty with hearts full of gratitude we left for the other village on our path through the forest, encountering several groups of monks, some of them Westerners, going to the temple or to seek instruction from their Lamas.

The next morning, the 4th of October, we left Daramsala to take up our pilgrimage again, and it wasn't until the 14th of October in the region of Katmandu that we were to meet more Tibetans. As a matter of fact, on that day we were received by Circon Rimpoche, an important person in Tibet who was in a state of atrocious depression because of what was going on in Tibet, according to members of his entourage whom we talked to: empty monasteries, obligatory marriage for the monks, and so forth. Circon Rimpoche was fifty years old. He looked about thirty and was very self-absorbed, suffering inside. Yet two or three times, his gaze brightened and he looked quickly at us. One of these glances destined for me particularly was more lively than the others. The divine essence of his inner being met what was in me for a few moments, and I sincerely hope that he got more strength and courage from our communion. How well I understood his state of mind then—forgetfulness of self in the crucifixion of love for others! On the afternoon of that same day we paid a brief visit to the Tibetan representative of the Dalai Lama, or so he was said to be. Our guide gave us some unfavorable information about him. That was our impression too, and so I would prefer not to pursue that meeting further. To make up for it, we were taken to a newly-built Tibetan monastery. We have many pleasant memories of time spent there with a twenty-five-year-old Tulku. Perhaps it would be useful for me to recall for some of you what a Tulku is. A Tulku is the reincarnation of a great Sage. One can be born into any family, but usually one is born into a family able to help him assume the pursuit of his mystical or spiritual work quickly. Among the Tibetans, a Tulku is usually recognized when he is very young, around the age of five or six. The trials are very difficult. He must point out objects that belonged to him in a previous incarnation all mixed up with many other things, and that is only one proof among others. A Tulku, naturally, grows up like a normal person. He plays, laughs, relaxes, and at the same time he is instructed and trained for the next step of his mission. When he begins it, he will still continue to be happy and appreciate relaxation. There is never anything stiff or formal about a true Sage, and there are especially no attitudes that could be taken as false pretenses. A Tulku is a Tulku during the exercise of his spiritual function. The rest of the time he provides an example of life lived in simplicity that is a witness to the divine in humankind. The Tulku who received us had the good humor of a child, while at the same time radiating great wisdom for whoever knew how to see it. Beside him was a German who lived with his wife and baby of eight months in Nepal, and who was staying in a nearby monastery, situated on the flank of a mountain. At the Tulku's request, he explained the Tankas (mystical paintings) of the magnificent temple on the first floor of the vast edifice where the Tulku lived. The time we spent there was so charged with mysticism that in writing these lines my whole being quivers again in gratitude and inner joy.

Later we met Tibetans in Darjeeling in the Himalayas, and in Gangtok in Sikkim, for which we had to get special visas. Here there is a story worth the telling. On the 19th of October we left Calcutta for Darjeeling by airplane because of a curious circumstance.

We had left our hotel in Calcutta at 10:45, and we were supposed to get to the airport about an hour later. There we learned that the plane was late. They told us that the plane might take off around four-thirty, but probably later. But the airport where we were supposed to land was ninety kilometers from Darjeeling, and so we would arrive by car at night. The first feelings of moodiness and disappointment passing, we just waited patiently. After all, there was nothing we could do, and finally at 3:30, later than expected, we finally left. On the airplane, a very well-dressed Tibetan, perhaps the only Tibetan on the airplane, sat down on my right and greeted me. My companion had already started reading. He was starting to read *The Land of White Clouds* by Lama Anagarika Govinda which I had just finished, and immediately the Tibetan took up a conversation in excellent English and the subject was almost immediately mantras (powerful words that you must repeat a set number of times in a special way). And I heard with surprise "I have a mantra for you! When you say it, you will be in contact with a powerful guru, whose name among the Tibetans is publicly known as Guru Rimpoche." I asked him whether he was speaking of the great Padmasambava, the celebrated guru of the past, or of Tomo Geche Rimpoche, who in his current incarnation is recognized as one of the most important authorities in modern Tibet. Lama Anagarika called him "a true Master of interior vision," and he added "To show the way (self-realization), and by his own example, to help others find it, that was the vital task of Tomo Geche Rimpoche." I was not forbidden to tell others about this mantra, and so I feel free to tell you about it, as I have already told so many others. Here is the mantra: *Oma Ahung Vaisa Pema Siti Hung.* The pronunciation of these old words cannot be fully explained; they must be experienced. This mantra must be pronounced 108 times in the morning and 108 times in the evening. I remind you that this mantra will establish an interior bond with a very powerful guru.

I interrupted my companion's reading, and he paid attention to the conversation. Our Tibetan said he regretted our brief sojourn in Sikkim where he himself lived. He proposed that we should come with him to that country, which he knew perfectly well, where we could meet a great Tulku, his cousin, and furthermore, he was happy to give us his address, which is rare for a Tibetan. This encounter might explain why our plane was late. Who knows? We were in the land of mystery and the contact may have exceptional importance for us and for others. Might it not be so for the mantra given to us that day that we have transmitted to you?

The trip from the airport serving Calcutta to Darjeeling was short. When we got there our guide was waiting, and she was a Tibetan. We soon learned that she was a believer and very religious, and during the four hours it took us to get to Darjeeling along the precipitous road winding through the mountains, which was so dangerous that it made for slow going, I told her about what we were looking for there, about our traditions, and in a few words, our reason for being. Our guide was struck by what she heard, and I felt confident. My intuition was right. She spoke to us about Mr. MacDonald who was in charge of the agency responsible for our stay there, and also for aid to the Tibetans. Mr. MacDonald, who is in reality Father MacDonald, a Canadian religious who has been in Darjeeling for years, is the director of St. Joseph's College in that high mountainous city. We were to meet him the next day on the 20th of October around eleven o'clock in the morning, and my first question, "Do you know our tradition?" made him laugh. "Do I know your tradition?" he answered, "I will soon be returning to our head office in Montreal in the main building of your Order there! I have seen your emblem in the building there, but I must say that I know nothing about your purposes and activities." I told him all I could about these matters and he appeared to be very satisfied. But you have to remember that coincidence, if indeed there is such a thing, is a curious thing! Wasn't there behind it all more proof of the attention of the All High from the beginning of our trip? Especially since the beginning of our trip? I don't doubt it for a moment. Father MacDonald had spent twenty years in Darjeeling. Had his long and frequent contacts with the Tibetans brought him to believe in reincarnation? It seemed so to me. At least, he seemed to have a largesse of spirit that was most remarkable and I understood why the local Tibetans were so attached to him. Father MacDonald was from a great spiritual tradition that is exactly the opposite of the fanatical religious intolerance whose unhappy and degrading presence is still, in our times of advanced intellectual and mystical civilization, seen in many countries.

Darjeeling is, above all, the city of mountains. And so there are a lot of jeeps, the only form of transportation appropriate to such bad roads. But Darjeeling has an impressive environment— such mountain views of snow-capped peaks against a sky of pure blue! In Darjeeling there are many Tibetans whom we met. We went along a precipice to a Tibetan village. There we saw Tibetans working, and they reminded us of the workers we saw making carpets and cloth in Daramsala. These tough people, so sweet and understanding and gentle, were hard workers. Their magnificent carpets were on sale for very low prices. In a very nice shop, my companion bought a good-looking jacket for ninety-five rupees, that is, about fifty-seven French francs. Of course he didn't ask for a reduction in the price. As I said, our guide was a young Tibetan with whom we got along very well. It was she who obtained the special price without being asked to do so. As a matter of fact, the Tibetans deserve our sympathy. They deserve it for what they are as a people, and equally because they are in exile. On that subject I don't share Father MacDonald's opinion. He maintained that the Tibetans were happier in exile than they had been back home in their feudal society where they didn't have the advantages that they had in India. However, we must recognize the fact that when and if the Tibetans go home again nothing will be as it was before because the young people have grown accustomed to a different way of life. As for saying that most Tibetan people prefer the kind of existence that they have in exile, I deeply doubt it. That night in Daramsala, we had just left the wise Lama who had invited us, and we heard someone running among the trees on the path behind us. One of the Lama's servants brought us a photograph of him surrounded by other monks. Tsering translated what was written on the back: "Keep this picture and help us go home!" I still have the photograph. And I pray for them...

We visited the very beautiful temple in the Tibetan village of Darjeeling where we meditated for a long time, forging new links with all that we had seen up to that point. In the afternoon of that same 20th of October we went to a Tibetan monastery to deliver a letter from Paris to a Lama schoolmaster. We were offered tea in a room where up until our arrival a Lama had been in prayer. We had a very interesting conversation with our learned hosts, thanks to the excellent translator who graciously agreed to be our guide. The most interesting part of that conversation concerned the Master Maitreya whom the Tibetans call Buddha Chamba. They expect him to come soon, and the Tibetans believe that he will come from the West, and he will be blond with blue eyes. So I raised a question, "The Christian West is waiting for Christ's return, the Druzes are waiting for their

Mahdi, you are waiting for the Master Maitreya. Isn't it reasonable to assume that there will be but one and the same Envoy for all?" And everyone present shared the opinion that I expressed. On the road returning to Darjeeling, our guide told us that some time ago a blond, blue-eyed American baby had been brought to the Tibetans by its parents, and its whereabouts were a secret, the reason why being the question. I asked "Do you think it is the Master Maitreya?" Our prudent guide answered "Maybe! We shall see." Truth, rumor? As our guide so wisely said: we shall see. That evening we were invited to meet our guide's family. We were magnificently received in the richness of their poverty. Precious mystical gifts were offered to us. But how cold I was in Darjeeling! There, once again my heart was experiencing fatigue, but I was too busy to listen to it.

We left by jeep for Sikkim at nine o'clock in the morning of the 21st of October. A few kilometers from Darjeeling we stopped at a temple to visit it. Afterwards our guide told us that it is so little known, even though it is not forbidden, that it is actually a secret temple. It is the temple of Maitreya. His statue is immense and was built many years ago by an inspired and enlightened Venerable Sage. The Master Maitreya is represented seated, which is unique among the Oriental temples where the Buddha and all the Sages are in the traditional lotus posture. The eyes are a deep, clear blue. The color of the face is a pale tint. It is really a Westerner who is represented in that place, a Westerner venerated with love by the Tibetans who go to that temple that is so hard to find. There my companion and I meditated for a longer time than usual, and I suppose that like myself he felt a communion with the divine, for which purpose we had gathered there. It was brief but dazzling. Before the Master, an invisible finger touched the center of my forehead and I felt the overwhelming dizziness of an exceptional cosmic contact. The fact that the Maitreya is seated is interpreted by the Tibetans as being a sign that his coming is near. He is ready to stand up. But that position, which is usual in the West, seems to confirm to me that the Master will come from the West. If memory serves, he also has his hands on his knees.

I will not persist in this *Letter from Nowhere* in writing about the Master Maitreya, but in the next I intend to remind you of the essential principles of Buddhism, to speak to you about Bodh-Gaya which is the Buddhist Mecca, where the Buddha experienced his enlightenment, and about Sarnath where he revealed his holy doctrine. I also intend to treat the circumstances of the Buddha and the Bodhisattva at the same time as I tell you more about the Master Maitreya. In effect, it seems to me necessary to approach the question of the future through the Master Maitreya. So much erroneous rubbish has been written about this subject which I consider a real sacrilege, and I believe that it is my strict duty to bring these matters down to just and holy proportions that are great and enlightening enough in themselves not to need any added superstitions or speculations. In the meantime I recommend the most extreme prudence. It would neither lead us forward nor help carry out the will of the Master. To hide behind error or to maintain it could even provoke a serious, guilty interference. In the next *Letter from Nowhere* I will deal with the Maitreya Buddha and I will tell you all that can be known on the subject. There will no longer be any questions or problems for you.

The road to Sikkim, as badly maintained as it is, traverses a magic countryside so sublime and beautiful that it is an enchantment in the real meaning of the term. It can't be described without diminishing its splendor. It is a mountainous countryside, everywhere green, a moving, vaulting greenness, yet everywhere dry like the boulders and rock gardens you seem to lose yourself in. That day was the last day of the festival of the goddess Durga. All the Hindus we met, men, women, and children, had colored rice stuck on their foreheads, as they had had for two days in honor of the goddess. When we had nearly reached Gangtok, after formalities all along the route, the jeep broke down, which amused us and gave us the opportunity to admire the exceptionally beautiful countryside again and watch the trucks full of laughing and singing adults and children who were enjoying the festival. There were a lot of soldiers in Sikkim! China is very near!

Just before Gangtok we turned off to the left eleven kilometers to Rumtek where Karmapa, who was then in France, has his home. We visited and greatly admired his temple. Karmapa has his meditation center there, and of course we ourselves meditated there before making a complete tour of the temple and admiring the one hundred small gold Buddhas that were given by the king of Nepal.

From Gangtok the view on the high peaks of the Himalayas is in the strongest sense of the term extraordinary. My companion and I enjoyed the unforgettable spectacle. Down below to the left was Rumtek and Karmapa's temple, and above on the far horizon were the snows illuminated by the setting sun! We were in a mysterious place, and nature herself had become mysterious. Invisible presences? Yes, they were there near to us, benevolent and welcoming us with love to teach us further about the powers of this world and the greatness of renouncement.

We needed the help of our guide to find the Lama who had been told of our arrival and who was to meet us. Diligently she did what was necessary. While the jeep was being repaired we went by car toward our arranged meeting place, but we met him along the way and he went with us. As customarily in similar circumstances, I immediately told him about our traditions. He himself gave me a number of useful explanations about Tibetan life, their devotion, and their profound beliefs. With him we visited the Tibetan temple of the Palace—the ground floor where the temple is situated and the second floor where we had access to very rare manuscripts that they had been able to save and bring to that place so that they could be preserved and studied. They contain thousands of years of wisdom. After that morning visit, the Lama offered us tea and cakes in a cafe in Gangtok in order to answer some of my questions. It was located on the second story of a house where we found peace and quiet. We had a conversation of the highest interest. I asked him a difficult question: "What is God?" His answer was an illustration of his profound wisdom. "The way of the Buddha is simple in regard to your question, and it contains an answer that will satisfy you. Consider this: When a house burns down, no one asks who built it. You try to save the people who live there." Then he told us about the three ways—Hinayana, Mahayana, and Varjayana, the latter being tantric and containing the danger of madness if there is no competent guru to instruct the person who chooses it. We talked about several other fascinating subjects, but I'll include them in the next *Letter from Nowhere* where they belong.

That morning the good Lama pointed out to us in the distance on the side of a mountain the monastery he was building with the funds he was able to collect. I don't know whether I will ever return to India. However, Tsering's holy and venerable Lama, responding to my question about whether I might be able, if I could arrange another visit to India, to meet the Dalai Lama, who was then on a prayer retreat, asked a servant for a pair of dice. He threw them on the little table in front of him. He stared at them for some time, and then he said "Yes, absolutely!"

In any case, if I'm able to undertake another trip there—and now I doubt it—I'll also visit Sikkim where many secret encounters have been promised. And I'll also see the completed monastery, the one being built by the excellent Lama who received us with so much goodwill. Now is this a coincidence, or another proof? The Lama was a friend of Phende Rimpoche who lives in Normandy and who is preparing his son to assume his succession when the time comes.

By comparison with that long encounter with Lama Kunga Yonten Hochotsang to whom our friend Gaby Genevet had recommended us, our visit to the Institute of Tibetology in the afternoon was much less interesting. When we were leaving the institute, which is really a small museum where you can buy books, brochures and interesting articles, we met our Lama again and spent a few more moments with him before separating with moving goodbyes. We learned a lot in Gangtok, but especially I had established as elsewhere solid bonds and powerful bases for an invisible edifice the majesty of which cannot be limited to this world. To end this letter about contacts with Tibetans I'll tell you an interesting fact. We made a lot of demands on our Tibetan guide. She had immediately cooperated with us without reserve, as had our other guides elsewhere, when I explained who we were and what we were looking for. But I felt that I myself would have to show her some proof. Waiting for the airport at Bagdoa, ninety kilometers from Gangtok, in the restaurant I revealed my intention to my companion, who answered me saying that I must do it. Then, I did something I practically never do, something I made a fundamental rule never to do: I told our Tibetan guide everything that I had read in her and her aura, and about her young brother who had accompanied us with our permission. Amazed, she took a photograph out of her bag and I told her how the people in the picture were related to her, indicating their personal problems and difficulties, as well as their pleasures and qualities. Finally, since she had just been chatting with a friend in a far corner of the room, I revealed to her the substance of what she had been talking about during that long conversation. Astonished by all the truths that I had just told her about, she exclaimed with admiration, "But you are a Lama, a Grand Lama!" And my companion was happy, but not surprised. "It was important to do that," he said simply. And just before we went into the room to have our luggage inspected, like everywhere in India, our guide and her brother came to say goodbye in the Tibetan manner, as I have already explained, by putting a white shawl around our necks. She looked at me again and said, "A Grand Lama," and we were separated. Thus, at Bagdoa, with our guide and her brother, our unforgettable encounters with the Tibetans were finished.

So here we are together again, my dear friends, by means of the *Letter from Nowhere,* and I hope that your interest has been served by the subjects I have written about relative to India. I have shared with you what has been for me a very rich experience. As I proposed in the first *Letter from Nowhere*, I express myself in each one in the way that a friend would write to his friends, that is, in all sincerity, sharing his impressions and the deepest feelings just as they are recalled without disguising any of them. When I shall have finished with the tale of my trip to India, and before writing to you about other countries that I have come to know—and there are a lot of them—first I will take up the important subject of our daily lives and the circumstances of our human existence. Which ones? I can't tell you yet, but, as you know, the choice is vast in these difficult but fascinating times that we are living through en route toward the greater light and peace of an era that has already begun.

So, in the course of our next meeting I will tell you about the state of being of the Buddha, the Bodhisattva, about Buddhism in general, and also about the Master Maitreya. Today, before leaving you, I would like to give you for your meditation a text that, no doubt, many of you are already familiar with, but which seems appropriate to conclude this letter and prepare you for the next one. It consists of an important excerpt that is called the *Sermon from Benares*, in which the Buddha gives the foundation of his teaching to his ascetic followers.

> "Here, Oh monks, is the mystical truth concerning the elimination of sadness: It is the complete cessation of that thirst, the renouncement, the deliverance, the detachment.
>
> "Here, Oh monks, is the mystical path that leads to the cessation of misery. It is the eight-fold way that includes right seeing, right intention, right words, right action, right way of life, right effort, ardent and just vigilance, and right samadhi (an ineffable mystical state).
>
> "Such is the mystic truth concerning suffering. Thus, O monks, my eyes have opened on all the things unknown

up to this day, and I now have knowledge, understanding, science, and illumination."

Finally, since we are to examine the Tibetan form of Buddhism, meditate upon this short citation from the celebrated Brug-pa Kun Legs of the Order of the Kargyupa, who lived towards the end of the fifteenth century of our era, because it is a prudent lesson useful in our time:

> "Authentic gurus are rarer than gold.
> Charlatans are more numerous than ants' nests."

I will leave you now, my dear friends, for a few months. We will be together again in October, for the last *Letter from Nowhere* of this year. In the meantime I send you my warmest wishes.

Very sincerely yours,
Raymond Bernard

8

OCTOBER 1978

The Bodhisattva and Tibetan Buddhism

Dear Friends,

    I propose today to tell you about Buddhism, and in particular about Tibetan Buddhism, along with the notion of the state-of-being of the Buddha and his followers, the Bodhisattva. I will also be referring to the future Buddha, whom I have mentioned in preceding letters. It is probable, if not to say absolutely certain, that many among you have heard of these topics. But so much has been written concerning them, with so many exaggerations, and with so many errors being committed, that my purpose is to try to correct these mistakes and bring forth this knowledge in its original purity which, after all, is infinitely more beautiful, greater and more impressive that all the rubbish that over the course of time—including our own time—has been excessively added, gravely deforming it and taking away from it its character of essential truth. So, even if in these pages I am led to treat points that you already know about, that will naturally serve as a simple reminder for you, but that reminder will finally include no commentary or argument having to do with anything but sure facts that are well established.

It was around 560 B.C. that the Buddha was born in Kapilavastu, which was the little capital of a state bordering on present-day Nepal, at the foot of the Himalayas. Because of his father, Suddhorade, he belonged to a noble caste, the Sakya family. Shortly after his birth, his mother, Maya, died and Siddhartha was raised by his aunt. Buddha Siddartha is also called *Gautama* or *Sakyamuni*, which means The silent one born in the Sakya clan. It was after his enlightenment or Awakening that he became known under the name of Buddha, that is to say the Awakened One, or as Bhagavant, the Blissful, or Jina, the Victorious. He started his quest for Nibbana, the Pali term for Nirvana, very early. His enlightenment is dated to the full moon of Vaisak (May) in 523 before our era. He was then thirty-seven years old. The Buddha died around 480 before Christ at the age of eighty. His death took place not far from present-day Patna, which my companion and I visited as well as the two most holy places of Buddhism. I'll tell you about these important visits a little later on. In our day there is no more doubt about the historical existence of the Buddha. As strange as it may seem, in spite of the numerous texts that have come down to us, it was at one time contested. There is nothing that ought to astonish us in that. Don't we see works appearing today proposing to prove that Jesus of the Christian tradition never existed, and that he was based on a historical person who was a bloody, pitiless revolutionary whose purpose was not messianic, but to liberate and bring about the deliverance of Israel and the usurpation of the throne for the benefit of his father and himself? However, these contentions are far from being new. The first writer to defend these ideas was Daniel Mass in a work entitled *The Enigma of Jesus Christ.* Certainly, it is necessary to concede that the historic Jesus that the Gospels speak about is hardly credible. There are too many facts and circumstances that don't square with what they call the reality of history. But to affirm, as some have done, that the evangelical Jesus never existed is going too far in drawing conclusions that themselves ultimately appear unrealistic. I assuredly do not want to get into any such debate where there can be no winner or loser. I will only observe that there are texts, the Gospels, that have inspired the religious and mystical life of multitudes for two thousand years, and that these texts, even beyond any religious sect, big or small, that may have appropriated them, and beyond all fanaticism, contain fundamental truths and an ideal way of life, with which you can inspire yourself to lead a just and correct life. And isn't that the point? From one perspective, of what importance is the question of whether Jesus existed or not, as long as the message of the Gospels can help those who receive it to better themselves? As for myself, I believe that these discussions on the subject of Jesus will quickly lose any importance for most of us. They are minor, secondary questions compared to the main message itself. But it makes you consider how strange it is that two great messengers, on whom were founded two religions that are among the most important of all time, should, at any time, see their historic reality contested. As it doubtless will be later on for Jesus, the Buddha's life henceforth is not the subject of any controversy.

Another parallelism can be found between Buddhism and Christianity, even though by the number of its adherents Buddhism considerably surpasses Christianity. The latter, born in Palestine, was spread elsewhere, leaving in its place of origin only a few historic sites. It was the same for Buddhism. Founded in India over two thousand five hundred years ago, it flourished there for fifteen hundred years, but almost entirely disappeared from that country between the eighth and twelfth centuries A.D. However, and we must add happily, from before the beginning of the Christian era, it was propagated outside its country of origin to spread over most of Asia. As I reminded you in the last *Letter from Nowhere,* Buddhism, in its diverse forms, is one of the most important religions in the world. But in India only .06% of the population practice it!

My companion and I visited in turn Sarnath on the 10th of October, and Bodh-Gaya on the 16th of October, with a side-trip to Nalanda on our way to Bodh-Gaya. Nalanda was a Buddhist university and convent center of great importance and prestige in the Seventh Century. It was on the 10th of October, after our morning visit to the Ganges to attend, at five-thirty, the rising of the sun and the worship service that is conducted by numerous devotees, then left at eight-thirty for Sarnath, which is located only ten kilometers from Varanasi (Benares). Sarnath is especially known for being the place where the Buddha gave his first sermon, the first part of which will always remain graven in stone. That is where he announced the doctrine of the Middle Way, which is the way between the satisfaction of our egotistical appetites and rigorous asceticism. It was there where the Eight Ways to the elimination of suffering were given. These ways lead to illumination, interior peace, beatitude, and finally to Nirvana. The first important convert to Buddhism, the emperor Maurya Asoka, had impressive stupas, or pagodas, built and a column on which were placed likenesses of lions that India had adopted as its emblem, and which were very evident in a nearby museum, the museum of Sarnath, one of the most beautiful in India, or so many people have told me. What you could call the age of Sarnath took place between the fourth and the sixth centuries, after the emperor Asoka, under the reign of the Guptas. In those days, fifteen hundred priests were in service every day by the banyan tree that was near the monastery of Vihara. This banyan tree, according to tradition, is just an ordinary tree, having nothing to do with the famous Bo-tree of Bodh-Gaya under which the Buddha meditated for years. Under that tree the Buddha purified himself before he received his enlightenment.

It was in the twelfth century that the decline of Sarnath began. A vast monastery had already been built there, by Queen Kumaradevi, but soon after the Hindu Masters of Varanasi (Benares) had the pagodas (stupas) demolished in order to get material for construction. Around the most sacred stupa, Akbar, the Moslem emperor had a brick tower built in order to commemorate his father's visit. The decline continued until 1836 when Sir Alexander Cunningham began some big excavations. The first discovery was a stone engraved with the Buddhist credo. Five other monuments were soon discovered, all from the Gupta period. The Dhamekh Stupa that had been built around 500 A.D., whose walls were covered with geometric figures, is the most important of the five from that era. On the same site they discovered a stupa in the Maurya style built of brick, much later than the others, dating from 200 B.C. The second monument was designed to hold relics of the Buddha. The emperor Asoka who built it and named it Dharmarajika. The sanctuary where the emperor would come to meditate is the third monument, the column of Asoka. The fourth and fifth are the chankama which stand for the sacred way the Buddhas followed in teaching his disciples. There is a big renaissance taking place in Sarnath right now, to coincide with the huge extension of Buddhism taking place in the world at the present time. In 1931 among the ruins of the seven former monasteries, the Mahabodhi association had a new one built near the Dharmarajika Stupa, which contains Buddhist relics brought from all over. A Japanese artist decorated the walls with murals depicting the main events of the Buddha's life. There is a magnificent collection of Buddhist literature in the Mahabodhi library.

In the temple containing the relics of the Buddha, my companion and I meditated for a long time, and since the temple was empty, we crossed the barrier that separated the choir of the building from the rest. In the choir was a splendid statue of the Buddha, the Master, around which many relics were scattered. And there in the ruins we followed the chankama, placing our feet where the Buddha once trod, all along the walk-way where he taught his followers. You understand, my dear friends, what such a pilgrimage means, and the profound emotion that we felt in such a place.

I promised earlier not to keep anything from you in relation to that trip, and so I will tell you about an experience I had on the 15th of October in Patna, the oldest capital in the world. The next day we were to leave for Bodh-Gaya, and we were visiting the city of Patna. At the Sikh temple, where the tenth guru was born there, we found the ambiance similar to that of the golden temple of Amritsar, except that in Patna the singing was done by women. My companion and I went out on a forbidden terrace to witness a magnificent sunset. Suddenly in the sun I saw very distinctly the Buddha sitting in the position we know so well and that is reproduced in his statues. Illusion? An image I created in myself? What I saw I saw quite distinctly, otherwise I would not have been able to look directly at the sun. I murmured to my companion "Look at the sun!" and if he didn't see it, he at least felt it. How valuable my companion was to me on such occasions! In Gangtok, at a Tibetan temple ignored by tourists to which our young guide had taken us, I felt suddenly possessed by signs that announced the experience. I closed my eyes and had just enough time to say to my companion "I'm going away..." and understanding that where I was going was beyond our physical environment, he positioned himself, I learned later, in such a way as to hold me up if he had to. The impression I felt in Patna seemed to be another sign on the evening before our trip to Bodh-Gaya, the cradle of one of the greatest religions in the world, the Mecca of Buddhism.

We left for Bodh-Gaya on the 16th of October at eight-thirty in the morning. The long and difficult road didn't permit swift passage. It was very hot, and we felt dispirited. No doubt that is how we had to earn the privilege that was ours to visit holy places where so few tourists ever go to see, as they are not included in general itineraries. On the road to Bodh-Gaya we stopped at Nalanda doing our best to commune with the glorious past perpetuated by that place.

Nalanda was founded after Bodh-Gaya, and quickly it became the center of Buddhist intellectual life, and a vast monastic complex where ten thousand monks and students lived was built. It is sad to learn that that university, taken for a fortress, was attacked in 1205 by looting Muslims who killed everyone who lived there and burned the immense library. Of the remains of Nalanda there is not much, but it is possible to imagine what it must once have been. The most important structure is the Great Stupa which is flanked by flights of stairs and terraces. A few votive stupas are still well preserved. Other sculptures can be seen in the Nalanda Museum. A center for Buddhist studies is housed in a recently-built building.

A dozen kilometers north of Bodh-Gaya is the city of Gaya which among the sacred cities of India ranks second, just after Benares. From all over India, in order to honor their deceased fathers and mothers, pilgrims come bearing funeral cakes called pindas, which are supposed to assure the peace of the souls of the departed. This offering is held to be essential for the souls of the deceased, freed from the bonds of earth, to go to heaven. Of course, this is a rite of the Hindu religion. The pilgrimage center is the temple of Vishnupada, built in the eighteenth century.

Finally we got to Bodh-Gaya where my companion and I experienced a powerful inner feeling of serenity and peace. That is actually where the Buddha, under the Bo tree, experienced his Enlightenment. That is where two thousand, five hundred years ago he rejected all the temptations of this world, he who with his status as heir to a prince was promised the highest fortunes. After the Buddha's death, some very important sanctuaries were established at Bodha-Gaya, but few of them remain. Nevertheless the Great Temple itself hasn't changed in at least a thousand years. Even in Bodha-Gaya you really feel like you're in another world. It is a solitary, wooded place on the banks of the Niranjana River. In the distance you can see a line of low hills.

You enter the sanctuary by way of the east door, and the torana of that door is covered with typically Buddhist sculptures. And then there is the Mahabodhi, a pyramidal tower sixty meters high. It is flat on top and crowned by a bell-shaped stupa. The

Mahabodhi was built in the seventh century, and it is very faithfully restored. A colossal gilded statue of the seated Buddha is placed inside the temple under a recess covered with garlands. In a room above you will find the statue of Maya Devi, the Buddha's mother. Some elegant stupas were built in the courtyard of the temple. These are Buddhist equivalents to Christian reliquaries. On the north side is the Sanctuary of the Promenade, which is an elevated platform on which are carved lotus flowers. When you walk west along this platform you arrive at the sacred Bo tree. It is worth noting that all the trees planted there for twenty-five hundred years are said to have come from the original Bo tree. Beneath the tree is the sacred seat. A balustrade two and a half meters high adorns the south and west of the temple. It is one of the most ancient remains in India. Its sculptures represent scenes from the life of the Buddha and episodes from mythology in which fabulous creatures and scenes of daily life are mixed together. On the south you will find the lotus basin where the Buddha was in the habit of coming to bathe. Bodh-Gaya is a holy place for both Buddhists and Hindus. Both communities share the administration of the temple. As I said in an earlier *Letter from Nowhere*, the Hindus recognize in the Buddha an incarnation of Vishnu.

You can easily conceive that Bodha-Gaya is the pre-eminently Holy Land and the place venerated above all by the Buddhists in the world. After a long period of austerity during which he would weigh the consequences of vanity, the Buddha put an end to that and entered meditation under a special tree that, as you know, is called the Bo tree, but whose exact name is Ficus religiosa. That's when he obtained Bodhi, that is, Awakening or Enlightenment. My companion and I appreciated not having an official guide there. That mistake by the travel agency was finally beneficial to us, as well as the fact that our driver could speak no other languages than his own. We were able to get a local guide who taught us a great deal, and who respected our intention to meditate in the most essential places, where we experienced unforgettable communion. These places were, of course, where the Buddha was enlightened. One of them was the precise spot, on a hillside seen from afar, where he remained for six years in meditation, with strict austerity. Our guide pointed it out to us. Another is where he accepted some milk and crossed the river to come to that place that has been known since then under the name Bodh-Gaya. It was truly there that the Buddha's message came to us across the centuries: *If you wish to pray in the noblest manner, take in your hand these three flowers—Contentment, Peace, and Justice.*

Now I must tell you about a new important fact to add to others already mentioned, that show how much our trip was controlled from On High, and you will understand why, when I remember our whole pilgrimage, my heart is filled with gratitude of the Masters who guided our steps and watched over our path. Actually, in Bodh-Gaya in addition to what was given us and what we felt so deeply within, we had the opportunity to visit a Japanese temple, speak with an authentic Zen Master, and attend a puja (ceremony). We received very much from these occasions. But especially, when we went to the Tibetan temple in Bodh-Gaya, we learned that it was consecrated to the future Buddha, He who is awaited, and I must say, He to whom during the course of our trip my constant thoughts were devoted appeared again on our journey. There in the monastery we spoke with two French people who were not very young. One was from Aix-en-Provence, and both of them had gone there to retire, to meditate, to learn, and possibly to awaken.

In order to make all of this perfectly clear, I must remind you of the fundamental elements of Buddhism, because it is from these basic facts that your understanding can be improved, and you can go further in putting together a comprehensive package of correct ideas. In addition, I'll try to be as succinct as possible without neglecting any important element.

Buddhism was in fact a revolt, the first, against the Hindu religion, which was in those days dominated by sacrifices and other powers of priesthood. For the man who was Prince Siddhartha, the true knowledge was a problem he had to resolve personally. He was very much taken with the suffering of this world: misery, sickness, old age. Giving up all the joy and promise of his life as a prince, he chose a wandering life, and to discover the way to wisdom, and real happiness, he chose at first to submit to the most extreme austerity. Meditation then brought him to adopt the Middle Way. Being Enlightened under the Bo tree, the Buddha began to teach new ideas. Everything, according to him, is destined to destruction. Any person who lives in this environment must suffer, knowing decline and finally death, and so the fundamental human experience is suffering. As long as a person doesn't give up his desires, the mental anguish that results from his preoccupation with material things corrupts his spirit, for which his body is a prison. There are some good acts that can permit him to raise himself and develop during the course of his birth and re-births. However, liberation from suffering can be obtained only by getting out of the cycle of birth and death, thanks to the passage to the other side, that is to say, Nirvana. The Buddha condemned extreme asceticism. He did not believe that asceticism could bring anyone to enlightenment. For the Buddha, there are four ways leading to enlightenment. The first is to awaken the heart and the mind, both of which are susceptible to outside attachments. The second admits that hatred and impure desires bar the way to enlightenment. The third is to free oneself from desire, ignorance, anxiety, and thoughtless habits. The fourth is a wholehearted attention to advance on the way to Nirvana, the highest purpose.

It was in Sarnath, which I spoke about before, that the Buddha finally converted five disciples, who at first had abandoned him because he had given up the practice of asceticism, and he sent them to various parts of India. He himself set about preaching the new teachings, and in order to do that he moved ceaselessly about until his death in 480 B.C. The Buddha rejected the authority of the Vedas and the caste system. Concerning himself only with the moral life, the Dharma, which he considered to be fundamental, he did not define divinity in any way. You will remember, my dear friends, the image recalled by the Lama we met in Gangtok: "When a house burns down, you don't ask who built it. You try to save the people who live there."

The Buddha preached a code of life much more accessible to the masses than the complexities of the Brahmins and the difficult statements of their Sages. He discouraged all adoration, but the needs of the people brought about the adoption of certain sacred symbols, and finally even the events in the life of the Buddha were represented in Buddhist art. In the centuries that followed, people who were used to worshipping gods and goddesses came to consider the doctrine of the Buddha to be too arduous and dry. And so it was that in the second century of our era, a schism came about, the result of which was two tendencies or schools—Hinayana, the Lesser Vehicle, and Mahayana, the Greater Vehicle. According to the Hinayana School, existence is too full of suffering and misfortune, and the only way to attain salvation lies in subjugating the Self, the only stable reality being Nirvana. The adepts of this school live mainly in Sri Lanka, Burma, Thailand, Laos, and Kampuchea. The cosmological structure of the Hinayana School does not include a Creator, but that does not mean in any way that they do not believe in His existence. Once again, when a house burns down... For the Mahayana School, the birth, enlightenment, and death of the Buddha were cosmic events, with all the importance that that implies, to the point that in the fifth century the Buddha was even worshipped as a divine being. Painting and sculpture give him a large place. As for Hinduism, as we have seen, it incorporated the Buddha as being an incarnation of Vishnu very easily, given its absolute tolerance of other religions.

My dear friends, if you are not Buddhists, or even if you are not very interested in Buddhism, this basic information will be sufficient for your understanding. But if you want to know more and study these great teachings more deeply, you should undertake to read some books that are true and moving studies. I recommend two books that Rosicrucian Editions can provide.

The first is a hard-cover book of more than five hundred pages entitled *Buddhism* (texts translated and presented under the direction of Lilian Silburn). The second title is *The Fundamentals of Tibetan Mysticism,* and the author is Lama Anagarika Govinda.

You surely haven't failed to notice all during the course of today's *Letter from Nowhere* the extraordinary parallel in their origins between Buddhism and Christianity. I have already explained this point, with examples. I should be able to add to them now the fact that emperor Asoka played a role in the recognition and spread of Buddhism in his day similar to that played by the emperor Constantine for Christianity. So, in the development of great religious movements, you can detect an underlying cosmic influence and plan. The fact that these movements eventually assumed the role assigned to them reveals the responsibility of humankind. As for the cosmic plan, it continues to develop, and it will continue to do so even if a rectification intervenes by way of reforms in these religions. If future changes seem to be irreversible, then new ways will arise, while the old ones will go on until they disappear completely.

In regard to what I formerly wrote on the subject of Christianity, in the newspaper *Figaro,* on Tuesday, the 9th of May, 1978, there was an interesting article by the well-known author Alfred Fabre-Luce entitled *"Something for Everybody to Read",* a review of a book by Hans Kung, published four years ago, but just published in French under the title *To be a Christian.* In the review he states:

> "We are no longer in an age that wants to know whether Jesus existed. For many decades Biblical commentators have said that even if they didn't contest his existence, they knew little about the course of his life. Contemporary research has gone far beyond this opinion. This research shows that in addition to what we know from the Gospels,

the witness of faith, more knowledge about the historical Jesus is possible to obtain. Scientific progress has made it possible for us to know more than our fathers did about Jesus and his times."

And further on Alfred Fabre-Luce adds "Jesus the man has evolved. He only learned about his mission little by little. He did not predict the future correctly (the end of the world that he predicted has not come to pass). His universalist message spread beyond the Jewish world only after his death. None of this should shock us because we can read about it in the Gospels and in the Acts of the Apostles. Other claims made by Hans Kung had already been made by the modernists, in the lifetime of Loisy. Then the church was successful in stamping them out.

Today this is not possible because the progress in communications is such that the results of research can be made known everywhere immediately. This is not something to regret. And how can we help but be in full accord with this writer when he declares, "After all, Jesus isn't an exclusive property of the Church, nor even of Christians." The same words could apply to the Buddha and to the Buddhists, but we have to recognize that from their point of view, because of the essential nature of Buddhism and its supreme tolerance, the problem could never be posed in the same fashion. But here we are concerned with Buddhism, and as interesting as are the parallels with other current religions, it is to Buddhism that we must address ourselves.

What we have to remember first of all is that which separates the Hinayana, or Lesser Vehicle, from the Mahayana, or Greater Vehicle. The Hinayana can be considered as the original tradition, not of the Buddha himself but of his disciples. Hinayana remains faithful to the original teachings and doesn't deify the Buddha, who is, after all, just a Grand Master. It seems to bring the wisdom of a mystical order to a purely intellectual knowledge, and its adherents are given over to discussion and speculation.

The result is that the initial intuition is veiled or even obscured, and the essential message of the Buddha is ignored. This is why after several centuries of existence, Buddhism appears to be an arid and confused doctrine. In our day Hinayana is always intellectualized, though it seems to have found again the spiritual and mystical vigor of its origin. It remains, nonetheless, the Lesser Vehicle, and so it does not go beyond the fundamental principles and the intellectual exegesis that arise from them.

At the end of the first century B.C. the Greater Vehicle was begun, the Mahayana. Some great mystics undertook to break the yoke, in effect, that the Lesser Vehicle had imposed on Buddhism. You should remember their names: Nagarjuna, Aryadeva, Asanga, Vasubandhu, Santideva. They gave force and vigor back to mystical practices, and in particular, they put the highest experiences of the Buddha back into the heart of Buddhist life. Another way to say this is that they recapitulated the experiences of the Buddha. Thanks to them, the Buddhist sources were regenerated and given new life. The strength of the Mahayana School lies in the fact that it knows and wants only to know the experience of the Absolute, and so it is in this perspective that it works. Moreover, it examines this experience and dominates it. It is simplicity and mastery. It goes quite beyond the relative.

For the Mahayana School, every man has the germ of the sublime experience of the Buddha within him. For the community of monks, it substitutes a universal community that is beyond time and space. The Mahayana is, to define it more exactly, a Buddhism of a new sort, that of the future Buddhas, the Bodhisattvas. Even the name Greater Vehicle signifies the Great Means of Progression. It should be noted that this newer Buddhism exists side-by-side with the older one. There is no conflict between them, and so there is no rivalry between Hinayana and Mahayana.

We have now come to the grand and inspiring subject of the Bodhisattva to which Tibetan Buddhism attaches such a high importance, since it is exclusive to the Mahayana School. It is only in understanding this subject perfectly that you can later begin to appreciate in all its worth in the person of the Maitreya Buddha. Otherwise you will fall into error and misunderstanding, into wrong notions, superstition, and dangerous traps. Let's look at what they understand by Bodhisattva within the Mahayana School. I think the best definition is that given by a celebrated representative of Singhalese Buddhism. Let us be attentive to it:

> "Buddhism is a doctrine that addresses itself to those who make an effort to liberate themselves personally, as well as to those who work not only for personal liberation but for that of others. Among us there are many who recognize the vanity of earthly pleasures, and who are certainly convinced of the universality of suffering, so that they take every opportunity to escape from the cycle of death and rebirth in order to gain liberation. There are others who not only observe experimentally, but actually experience all the suffering of the world. At that point their love is limitless, and so penetrating is their compassion that they renounce their own liberation in order to devote their lives to the sublime purpose of service to humanity as well as to their own improvement. That is the nature of the noble purpose of Bodhisattva. This ideal of the Bodhisattva is the purest and most beautiful ever proposed to the world. What could possibly be more beautiful than a life of perfectly pure, disinterested service? The ideal of the Bodhisattva is an exclusively Buddhist teaching."

But you must not suppose that service to others should cause you to slow down or diminish your efforts toward the highest ends. The greatest Tibetan saint, Milarepa, gave important advice on this subject:

> "You must not be too zealous or too reluctant in your intention to serve others before you yourself have realized the Truth. Otherwise, it would be like the blind leading the blind. As long as there is a heaven, there will be no lack of beings receptive to those in need and each will find their opportunity. To that end, I exhort each of you to swear to a unique resolution, which is to attain to the Buddha state for the well-being of all living beings."

But I think that it is the Lama Anagarika Govinda who gives the most useful advice on the subject of the Bodhisattva. He writes "These (the highest virtues of a Bodhisattva) do not only consist in avoiding that which is bad, but to cultivate the good through acts of abnegation, love, and compassion, aroused by the flames of universal suffering, in which the unhappiness of others is felt as your own. A Bodhisattva does not seek to teach others, except by his own example, and he pursues his spiritual career without losing sight of the well-being of others like him. That is how he ascends to the highest end, and how he inspires others to do the same." The Lama continues, "While making progress on our own way, no sacrifice we undergo for the love of others is made in vain, not even if it is misunderstood or simply used by its beneficiaries. Every sacrifice is an act of renunciation, a victory over ourselves, and so, consequently, an act of liberation. Whatever is the exterior result, it brings us closer to our goal."

The wish of the Bodhisattva is expressed by all those who wish to follow the sacred path of the Enlightened One, of the Buddha. Here it is:

> "I take upon myself the weight of all suffering. I resolve to accept everything. I will not turn my back. I will not run away. I will not worry. I will not abandon anyone. I will renounce no one. And why? Because the liberation of all beings is my vow. I work for the installation, among all beings, of the incomparable kingdom of knowledge. It is not only with my own liberation that I am occupied. I must

contribute to pulling all beings out of the ocean of Samsara (the cycle of births and deaths), by means of the vehicle of perfect knowledge. I must pull them out of the deep ravine of calamity and have them cross the current of becoming. I myself must put an end to the innumerable sorrows of other beings. Right to the very end of endurance I must bear all degrees of suffering inherent in the misfortunes one meets in all the different worlds. And no being should be deprived of a share of my goodness. I have resolved to live for unaccountable periods in every sorrowful destiny. In that way I will help all beings to liberate themselves from whatever destiny they find themselves in, in whatever world that might be. Because it is better for me alone to put up with sorrows so that other beings might not be plunged into sorrowful states. In all these states-of-being, among animals, with the king of death, in the jungle of hell, I will become a hostage in order to be a hostage for the whole world. I wish I could take into my body the multitude of all suffering for the well-being of everyone. For all beings, in their best interest, I guarantee that I give my word in truth. I am worthy of faith, I do not break my promises. I will never abandon all these beings. Why should I? Because of the highest hopes of my heart for omniscience, whose purpose is to free everyone. For I have not undertaken my search for the perfect and incomparable Awakening in the desire for pleasure, nor to enjoy the qualities of the five desires, nor to give myself up to the joys of the sensual domains. I am not proceeding with my career as a Bodhisattva in order to obtain the mass of pleasures from the world of desires."
(*Vajradhvaja-Sutra*, excerpts)

I could carry on at length, at great length, about the grandeur of the Bodhisattva and the way it has chosen to follow. The explanations given up to this point have certainly shown—and with a good deal of evidence—that the Bodhisattva is, above all, a group with infinite compassion, which, while pursuing its own evolution towards the Awakening, the Accomplishment—in a word the Enlightenment and the Buddha-state—foresees in doing this not only their own personal ends but also, in the spirit of the absolute gift of themselves, the same for all other beings in every world. The way that they have chosen is, naturally, Buddhism, that is, the acquisition of the state of Buddha-ness, and from the beginning they give the same veneration to the Three Jewels comprising the Buddha, the Law (Dharma), and the Community (Sangha); the Buddha because he discovered the holy truths and is thus omniscient; the Law because it is the doctrine and discipline that He established; the Community or Sangha since His time has taken on a much larger meaning and now includes all those, religious and lay, who adhere to Buddhism and its Three Jewels, saying three times: "I take my refuge in the Buddha. I take my refuge in the Law. I take my refuge in the Community." You cannot consider yourself a Buddhist without taking this refuge. In the remarkable book entitled *Buddhism* that I mentioned earlier, the author gives the following beautiful explanation: "For beings who are suffering, the Buddha is the doctor who knows sickness and its causes; the Law is the remedy that cures it; the Community is the nurse who administers the medicine." You should note that the Buddha, the Dharma, the Sangha, and rules of morality form the four fundamental qualities of the Saints who have attained Nirvana. Their are six, eight, or ten subjects, according to traditions, on which the disciple must meditate, and the Three Jewels always come first. In order, these subjects are the Buddha, the Law, the Community, the rules of morality, the gift, the divinities, the inhaled and exhaled breath, the elements of the body, and tranquillity. Finally, to understand these fundamental questions you must know that there are three levels: the ordinary Man, the Arhat (or disciple), the Bodhisattva, and the progression goes from one to the next. Any step may take centuries. Metaphorically, whoever has experienced the Buddha's earthly Enlightenment has become a Bodhisattva.

Over the course of time there has been more than one Buddha. The best known is actually the Buddha Sakyamuni, and He is the one we generally refer to because He is the most recent. Similarly, there is no single Bodhisattva, but a large number of them. The Mahayana in this world is visible as the Reality in the heart of all beings. It is in this world that you can see its triple greatness. You can know the greatness of essential being, of immutable, undifferentiated Reality, the greatness of the attributes revealed in the person of the Buddha, and the greatness of the actions of the Buddha and the Bodhisattvas in their benevolent works. An essential point to note, according to the Buddhist tradition expounded by Subhuti, is that "Neither the Buddhas nor the Bodhisattvas receive Enlightenment through invariable teachings, but rather through a natural, spontaneous, intuitive process." We could go on at great length about the qualities and indescribable greatness of the Bodhisattvas. Whole books, in fact, wouldn't be sufficient, and this subject, that of the Compassionate Ones, is extremely moving. Perhaps my role should merely have been to draw them to the attention of those who had never heard of them or who had never learned much about them. They are now familiar with one of the greatest spiritual subjects that exists, and if the occasion arises they can study more deeply. In any case, it was all the more important that I speak to you about it as my intention is to conclude this *Letter from Nowhere* with the Master Maitreya and the fact that the future Buddha of humanity, is now, and will be until the accomplishment of his mission on earth later, a Bodhisattva. But beforehand I'd like to tell you briefly about another topic, that of Tibetan Buddhism.

Tibetan Buddhism could more accurately be called Lamaism, because of the way it is organized. And Alexandra David-Neel doesn't hesitate to call it that in works published during her lifetime, which are recommended by Rosicrucian Editions. In spite of my great admiration for the great person Alexandra David-Neel was, I don't share her opinion on this point. She died at the age of one hundred and one, and after her death, some texts that I judge to be apocryphal, were published. At least, they do not contain the ultimate conclusions to which she had come. There is no point in qualifying Tibetan Buddhism as Lamaism. It's true that it has taken a particular shape in its organization, but that doesn't make it in any way less truly Buddhist in every respect and in the strictest sense of the term. They hold tightly to the tenets of Mahayana Buddhism. In Tibet, as elsewhere, but more powerfully there because it is the country where the Mahayana is imposed the most. The Mahayana has been able to include a great diversity of orientations that, I must reiterate, are not in competition with each other. On the contrary, these orientations, including Tantric Buddhism, work in the most perfect harmony. A quotation from Lama Anagarika Govinda is appropriate here. It is an extract from his magnificent work *The Fundamentals of Tibetan Mysticism*, where you will find the notion of the Bodhisattva. If you meditate on this quotation, my dear friends, it will help you understand Buddhism in its entirety. But listen to the wise Lama:

"The universality of Buddhism at first seems to be a confusing multiplicity of religions or philosophical schools, until the moment when in the Mahayana (the Greater Vehicle), which is vast enough to allow diversity of orientations and ideas as necessary forms of expression of different temperaments, or degrees of knowledge, it can raise itself to the level of a conscious principle. That is achieved by the placing in evidence of the ideal of the Bodhisattva that holds up the image of the Buddha as the highest realization of the Buddhist effort, even the center of the religious life. Whatever you have to say about the reality or unreality of the world and its connection with spiritual experience, or about the subject of the state of liberation and about the definitive Nirvana, one thing remains firm—the state of Accomplishment, of Enlightenment, of Buddhaization, has been attained before and it is possible for any human being to attain that same state and through the same way. On this point all the schools are in accord. This way, moreover, is not one of evasion, but rather one of victory over the world by increasing knowledge, by an active love for your neighbor, by deep participation in the suffering and joy of others, and by equanimity when faced with the pleasant and the unpleasant. This has been amply illustrated by innumerable previous existences of the Buddha (up until the last as Guatama Sakyamuni) such as are reported in the jatakas, the history of previous births. And even if we don't care to attach historical value to these tales, nonetheless they show the concept of basic Buddhism and the idea, common to all Buddhist schools, of the ways to the development of a perfect Enlightened One. In the *Tipitaka,* Pali canonical Buddhist writings, later known as *Theravada, the Teachings of the Ancients,* which is predominant in the Buddhism of southern countries, we can distinguish three types of Liberated Ones. First, there is the Saint, or Arahan, who has finally vanquished the illusion of the ego and its suffering, but who, however, doesn't have the innate knowledge nor the consciousness of an omnipresent Enlightenment that can contribute not only to his own Enlightenment, but also to that of innumerable other beings. Second, there is the Private Enlightened One or Pacceka-Buddha who possesses, in effect, the omniscience of the Buddha, but lacks the means to communicate it. And finally, there is the Sammasam-Buddha, the Completely Enlightened One, who is not only a saint, a savant, and an Enlightener, a Perfect, an All-Developed One, a being in whom all spiritual capacities have reached their maximum, their perfection, their maturity, their complete harmony, and whose knowledge embraces the universe. Such a being cannot be identified within the limits of the individual personality, within the character or individual existence. Of him you may rightly say: 'No measure fits him. There are no words to speak about him.' It seems that originally the Arahan, the Pacceka-Buddha, and Sammasam-Buddha were simply classed as types or states of Accomplishment. But according to Buddhist precepts a human being is not created once and for all with dispositions and characteristic properties that cannot be changed. On the contrary, he is what he makes himself. The knowledge of these three possibilities leads necessarily to the formulation of three ideals, and from that point of view he cannot possibly doubt that the ideal of the Perfectly Enlightened One is the highest. Since this ideal is sufficient to allow innumerable beings to cross over the ocean of this ephemeral world (samsara) and reach the shores of Liberation, it was called Mahayana, the Greater Vehicle. The other ideals (in particular that of Arahan) in which individual and personal liberation are on the first level were called Hinayana, the Lesser Vehicle.

"The designations Mahayana and Hinayana were first consecrated at the council of King Kaniohka in the first century of the Christian era, when the different ideals and paths to Liberation were discussed and defined by the leaders of the different schools. The result was that the ideal of the Mahayana was the only principle large enough to tie together the diversity of all the kinds of Buddhism. There is nothing astonishing in the fact that the majority of the participants in the synod pronounced themselves in favor of Mahayana, or that the minority groups, opting for the Hinayana, soon disappeared. Furthermore, the Theravadins, who didn't attend the council, presumably because they no longer lived in continental India, strictly speaking can't be identified with the Hinayana because they don't reject the ideal of the Bodhisattva."

These explanations are the most fundamental ones, and whoever wants to have certain and serious facts about Buddhism should remember them. In regard to Tibet, however, we must not lose sight of the fact that the Mahayana or Greater Vehicle took its proper shape there. It is, as a matter of fact, an amalgamation of Indian Tantric Buddhism, and it absorbed into itself many other older beliefs. Since the Tibetan exile, it is this form of Mahayana that is perpetuated in those parts of India where Tibetans live. But this same form, which, as I previously stated, some people call Lamaism, exists also in Mongolia, in Sikkim, which my companion and I visited, and in other neighboring regions. But it was around 750 A.D. that Lamaism began to take its present form with the coming to Tibet of the Guru Padmasambhava, a name that you should also remember. That's when the typically Tibetan Buddhist tenets were elaborated little by little, most of them being translated from Sanskrit. Since the fourteenth century they have consisted of two large collections of three hundred and twenty-five volumes containing four thousand, five hundred and sixty nine texts—the Kanjou, with teachings attributed to the Buddha, and the Tanjour, containing commentaries. And it is surprising to learn that these two collections do not contain all the Tibetan Buddhist works! Another important point to note is that Tibetan Buddhism comprises several schools that are practically doctrinally the same, differing only in the accent put on such and such a point or practice. Very summarily defined these schools are the following—the school of the Nyingmapas, the oldest, which is connected to Padmasambhava; the school of the Kargyupas, whose origins go back to Marpa and his disciple Milarepa who lived in the eleventh century, as well as to some Tantric Yogins who came from Bengal; and the school of the Gelugpas, which means "those who follow the works of virtue." This last school was founded by Tsongkhapa, who lived in the fifteenth century.

He reformed Tibetan Buddhism, with very few changes, in order to create his Order. The monks of this Order wear yellow caps in order to distinguish themselves from those who belong to older schools who wear red caps. That's the order that the Dalai Lama has belonged to since the fourteenth century.

All this information is essential, and I wouldn't give it to you or remind you of it in this survey of Buddhism, without sending you on to other exciting books in order to learn more about it, for it is evident that here in a *Letter from Nowhere* that is relatively brief in regard to the size of the subject matter, I can't touch on all the details. I am happy to have broken this ground with you and for you. It's up to you to decide to dig deeper still for your own interior benefit. It's a point, however, on which I must insist. It was my companion who emphasized it on our return by asking "In the final analysis, is there anything over there that we don't have in the West?" And he was absolutely right. The authentic tradition was slowly developed over the course of time in diverse forms adapted to different civilizations. And so the West already has at its disposition, in forms that are accessible to it, all that is useful to it in order to attain the states or an evolution corresponding to the state of the Buddha or the Bodhisattva, for example. The terms are different, but they stand for ideas that are identical. It is necessary to constantly remember that when comparing formulas or expressions. You must remain firmly grounded in your own way while learning what is being done elsewhere for the same purpose. In doing this, you will be assured of not ending up with extreme interior confusion or even dangerous disorder, going ceaselessly from one doctrine to another, or from one experience to another. From the point of view of spiritual research, such behavior would be a failure, and maybe for some simply an attraction to exoticism, an attraction wrongly compared to an interior quest. It would be, in any case, a waste of time in regard to the goal to be reached.

Now I come to the last topic of this *Letter from Nowhere*, which is the Bodhisattva Maitreya, the future Buddha of our world, He who is Awaited, the Master and Teacher, whom, consciously or unconsciously, every man and woman on our earth is waiting for in their hearts.

As I have already said, and it's not useless to repeat it many, many times, the exciting subject of the Master Maitreya has given rise to exaggerations, to hypotheses and stupidities that are, in regard to such an important question, a true sacrilege. To give a simple example, even though the future Buddha Maitreya is not yet incarnated on the physical plane, some authors—it would be better to call them inventors—haven't hesitated to describe his physical appearance, and many of them become unconscious accomplices, but accomplices all the same, in spreading this false information by comparing it to an act of faith. That is certainly not the way to become a servant of truth! At the very best, they made themselves the mouthpieces of people we would not hesitate to call inept. Some of them demonstrate an irresistible attraction to the most extravagant suppositions. They are entranced by the marvelous, even if the marvelous is only fantasy, and they prefer it to the plain truth because the truth is less mysterious. If they only gave themselves up to this attraction to mystery and those ideas, that would be a worse evil, because the day will come when they'll have to rectify their mistakes and adopt a point of view that is more just. But if by misfortune, urged on by I don't know what motives, or in good faith letting themselves be used as toys by obscure forces, they have spread these false notions around, it is clear that they have taken on a heavy responsibility that will have karmic consequences for them. That is why, dear friends, I must put you on your guard and exhort you to the most extreme prudence. Do not necessarily believe whatever might be said to you on this topic or about the Masters in general. Always remember the famous injunction from the *Book of Tao*, "Those who know do not speak, and those who do not know speak." So make careful choices in your reading, and before accepting whatever from whomever, think deeply and don't let yourself be convinced right off. In regard to this matter, it is better to refuse categorically to adhere to one thesis over another, for you might be led into grave error that later would be difficult to get out of.

These necessary reservations having been stated, here is what the purest and most authentic traditions allow to be said about the Master Maitreya. It will perhaps seem to be very little to those who are drawn towards mystery and extravagance, but it will greatly serve as the basis for meditation and cosmic contact. In any case, truth is sufficient unto itself.

I will not repeat what a Bodhisattva is since I went over this subject in the preceding pages, but Maitreya is a Bodhisattva, and you know what that represents and means.

In the name Maitreya, there is the word Maitri that means All Love. Maitreya, the future Buddha, is actually the Very-Loving and the earthly reflection of Amoghasiddhi in human personification. Amoghasiddi is the Dhyani-Buddha, personifying the Wisdom that accomplishes all works. He is "the Dhyani-Buddha from the northern part of the sky, and he represents to some degree the midnight sun, which is to say the mysterious activity of spiritual forces, which beyond the senses, hidden and invisible, are working to bring beings to the maturity of knowledge and deliverance. The yellow light of an interior sun (Bodhi) plus the dark blue of the night sky (in which the unfathomable space of the universe seems to open) together form green, the calm mysticism of Amoghasiddhi." What is essential is that Amoghasiddhi incarnates all-accomplishing Wisdom that frees us from karma. In it is included that supreme freedom in which the Enlightened One goes into the world without causing new karmic attachments, that is to say, without forming new desires, or formative forces or attitudes. Amoghasiddhi transforms these forces in the cauldron of all-embracing love and mercy, impelled by a non-egotistical, enlightened savior. He is the fifth Dhyani-Buddha, that is, one of the five Supreme Lords of eternal Wisdom, and the fact that he is the fifth does not mean that he is inferior to the four others. Like the other four, the famous mantra OM MANI PADME HUM holds him in check and acts through him. Finally, Amoghasiddhi is the Lord of the Great Transformation whose vehicle is the winged man, the man in transition toward a new dimension of consciousness. In him the interior and the exterior become one, fusing together. The physical becomes the psychical, and vice versa. But, if you look around you and you consider what is happening on the human and planetary scale, you will perceive the reign of Amoghasiddhi, and, as I have said, the Maitreya Buddha in the earthly reflection of Amoghasiddhi. In other words, he expresses and manifests on earth the fifth Dyani-Buddha, one of the Supreme Lords of our universe. This is to point up the importance of Lord Maitreya in the function he must fulfill in the service of humanity.

My dear friends, in putting all this together in this *Letter from Nowhere*, this information about Buddhism, about the Buddha and the Bodhisattva, about the notes on the Lord Maitreya and Amoghasiddhi, you will surely have the best, absolutely precise, bases on which to meditate. Remember that it's up to you to find greater illumination from your knowledge of the Master Maitreya. You will get it in proportion to your preparation for it, and no one will ever be able to interpret for you what you have received. Note this well: no one now in the world can pretend to be the chosen disciple of Maitreya. But it is written that when the time comes those whom he will use will come, on the one hand, from people already engaged in service to a spiritual or initiatic order, and, on the other hand, from those who are properly prepared. Any other notion is only a dream, an illusion, a fantasy. Besides, the Master Maitreya will not necessarily surround himself with disciples. He will act, as he's already acting, through those I just spoke about without their necessarily knowing that they are performing such a service. But an opportunity to serve will be entirely missed if one is content to wait or to prepare oneself otherwise than by fulfilling the work to which one is consacred or pursuing in oneself.

The expression I'm now going to use is very strong, and I beg you to excuse me, but it makes its point perfectly: the Master Maitreya will never need bigoted, intolerant people. He needs, and he will need seekers who, where they are and in what they do, are capable of the utmost fidelity and loyalty without reserve or restriction, because it is in whatever they do and wherever they are that they will transmit the energy of the Very-Loving Master, without having to refer to him. His service requires and will require reserve, discretion, and selflessness, surpassing of the ego, and silence. So, in pursuing your progression in your spiritual research, know and remember that you are on the right track toward what is expected of you, and that when the moment comes, in this life or another, you will be counted among those who served and still serve the Sublime Master, the Lord Maitreya. In sum, the only thing asked of you is for you to remain what you are in the intention of your spiritual path. Any other attitude, in particular to intellectualize the sublime subject of the Master Maitreya, or to place him on the level of emotion and sentimentality, would constitute a regrettable error, both for this subject as well as for yourself. To be where you are, to serve where you are, that's the best and greatest preparation.

To end this *Letter from Nowhere,* I would like to cite three texts. The first was inspired by the Lord Maitreya of Asanga, and it has to do with a description of the dhyana (absorption of energy, ecstasy, meditation). It consists of a simple, short text. Asanga lived at the end of the fourth century. He was the founder of the Yogacara or Vijnanavada school. The second is an address from Vimalakirtinir of the Asutras, and the third is an extract from the *Sutra of the Perfect Awakening,* which comes from around the seventh century. The purpose of this sutra is to demonstrate the double tendency of the Mahayana, or Greater Vehicle: Look only to Awakening, and its Revelation; open yourself to all beings without exclusion. Different Bodhisattvas speak on this subject to the Blessed, to Buddha, and he answers them. Among them is the Bodhisattva Maitreya. These are the words and answers that will be cited. These very ancient texts show that the future Buddha, the Master Maitreya, was already well known many centuries ago, and he is working still in today's world. That fact did not lead any of those great Sages of former days to forget their own duties and service, and rely only on a hope, however great it was.

Here are the three texts:

The Lord Maitreya of Asanga

Immobility of the heart in pure interiority, founded on the vigilance and energy that create the fruit of happiness in universal harmony, causes supernatural understanding and Brahmanic structures. With the ecstatics it is three times the greatest of virtues. May the Sage who understands the absorption of psychic energy give himself over to it with ardor. In every way, the songs of the Buddha have realized the absorption that abounds in Samadhi (an ineffable mystical state). Spending their days in the great happiness of absorption, however, they come to be re-born in lower states (Note: the sons of the Buddha is an expression that refers to the Bodhisattva). With the help of this same absorption they lead all beings toward the triple Awakening. Then, being in possession of this Knowledge, they have established an inexhaustible ecstasy in this world.

The Vimalakirtinir of the Asutras

Reverend Maitreya, at the moment when you arrive at the supreme and perfect Enlightenment, all other beings, will also arrive at the same Enlightenment. Why? Because this Enlightenment has already been acquired by all beings. Reverend Maitreya, when you are in complete Nirvana, all beings will be in complete Nirvana. Why? Because there is not a single being who has not already pre-Nirvanaed. Seeing that all beings are originally at peace and in Nirvana, the Buddha told them the true way of being, the parinirvana.

No one approaches it or draws away from the Bodhi (Awakening, Enlightenment). Do the same for us, Oh Reverend Maitreya, that these sons of gods may reject these imaginary views of the Bodhi. The Bodhi is the coming together of every tradition. The Bodhi is the end of thinking. The Bhodi is the rejection of all false views. The Bodhi is outside unrest, disquiet, and agitation. The Bodhi is the cessation of desires. The Bodhi is peace because it rejects all quarrels and adherence. The Bodhi is non-duality because there is no object of thought or mind in it. Being without origin, or length, or disappearance, or modification, it is beyond any conditions. The Bodhi, exempt from the passions of reincarnation and all their unpleasantness, is not comprised. The Bodhi exempt from possession and rejection is without waves.

The Sutra of the Perfect Awakening
(Then the Bodhisattva Maitreya arose, greeted them, and said:) Oh, all compassionate Blessed Ones, how must you cut the root of becoming, you Bodhisattvas and other beings who will live in a decline of the Doctrine, who desire to struggle in the ocean of the great extinction of Tathagata (the highest designation of a Buddha). How many ways are there of becoming? How many ways is it possible to seek the Awakening of the Buddha? How many saving graces must the Bodhisattvas who enter the world anew have in order to convert and educate other beings? Oh, please do not give up your immense compassion that leads you to save the world! Lead all the practicing Bodhisattvas and other beings who will live in a time of the decline of the Doctrine to acquire the eye of pure wisdom, to polish the mirrors of their consciousness, and to awaken completely to the unsurpassable knowledge of Tathagata.

(Then the Blessed One said)

Sons of the family, through all eternity all beings err in becoming as a consequence of all sorts of attractions and desires. The different kinds of beings, however they come into the world—from eggs or placentas, from humidity or through apparition—come to life because of sexual desire. Know that the fundamental root of desire is desire. Births and deaths go on without end because all sorts of desires stimulate attraction. The origin of attraction is desire, and the origin of life is desire. Life and the attraction of beings for each other rest fundamentally on desire. Desire born from attraction is the cause, life issues from that attraction is the fruit. Favorable and unfavorable elements come from different states of desire. If the state is contrary to what you like, your conscience engenders feelings of hatred and rancor, which in turn create all sorts of karmic acts. These then result in a rebirth among the half-starved phantoms or in the underworld. Know that to renounce attraction and the path of Karman (karma) is a desire. Renouncing evil in order to love the good gives you rebirth in the world of the gods or of men. Know as well that the renunciation of evil is yet another form of attraction, and that the abandonment of attraction as well as rejoicing in this detachment have attraction as a foundation, producing excellent and superior results. But all of this that proceeds from becoming and is not the fulfillment of the Holy Way. This is why those beings desirous of detaching themselves from becoming and rebirths must first break away from covetousness and eliminate their thirst for attraction.

Sons of the family, the Bodhisattvas who appear in the world do not do it by attraction, but by benevolence and compassion, in order to guide others to detach themselves from attraction. They enter into becoming, stimulating all sorts of greed. All the beings who live in the time of decline of the Doctrine and will be capable of abandoning their desires, of eliminating hatred and attraction, will break away forever. Searching assiduously for the domain of perfect Awakening of Tathagata, they will awake to purified consciousness.

Sons of the family, it is uniquely through the saving grace of the great compassion that the Bodhisattvas enter the worlds and perfect those who are not yet awakened. They go in favorable and unfavorable circumstances, manifesting themselves in all sorts of ways, in order to transform beings and guide them to the accomplishment of Buddhahood. They are supported by the strength of their pure vow, pronounced for all eternity.

It is easy to understand the importance of these ancient texts, new and always so pertinent to our lives, in particular the last one, because the question of the Master Maitreya is fundamental, and the answer of the Benevolent, of the Buddha, is very revealing. I am persuaded that a long, repeated meditation on this last text will be a source of joy and great inner understanding.

So this is the end, my dear friends, of this *Letter from Nowhere*. As I said previously, it will no doubt be harder to understand than the others, by reason of its subject matter. I made an effort, however, to give you just the essential facts, so that you can pursue whichever topic interests you personally, if you wish to do so. The purpose of this *Letter from Nowhere* was to remind you what is necessary to learn. If you wish to know more on these subjects, let me give you a little advice. Choose carefully what you read and how you read it. I have suggested in these pages what books seem to me to be the best and most useful. Others will be published by the Rosicrucian Editions, and I assure you that my choice of them was made very carefully in order to avoid any confusion and to enlighten you without sending anyone down useless paths.

Having told you of the future Buddha, Master Maitreya, I will quote an evangelical sentence that remains excellent advice, especially in these times of disorder, but also in these times of great hope rising among humankind. "There will come days when ye will long to see one of the days of the Son of Man and shall not see it. And they will say unto you Lo there! and Lo here! Do not depart and do not pursue. For just as the lightning flashing out of the one part under heaven unto the other part under heaven shineth so shall the Son of Man." (Luke 17)

So as always, let us remain open while being constantly cautious.

>Very sincerely yours,
>Raymond Bernard

About CIRCES International, Inc.

CIRCES is a vehicle for the expression of a New Spirituality in today's world. By providing tools, resources, encouragement, and guidance to its members, CIRCES creates an environment in which the serious student may develop and realize the fullness of his or her innate potential. In encouraging and promoting research into the common roots of the World's Cultural and Spiritual Traditions, CIRCES also contributes to the expression of love, tolerance, understanding, and altruism among the various peoples of the world and thereby fulfills its mission.

As an International Circle of Seekers and Doers, CIRCES is open to all sincere aspirants—without regard to language, ethnic origins, religion, gender, or political persuasion—who are dedicated to the ideals of World Peace and the reduction of Human Suffering through effective integration of the spiritual and scientific technologies. Accordingly, members of CIRCES are not content to study and reflect but are motivated as well to act constructively within their immediate cultural and social environments.

Although CIRCES presents itself as a fraternal movement of spirituality and initiation, it teaches neither doctrine nor dogma but, instead, presents techniques whereby each member may awaken to the Teaching which already resides within him or her. In this, CIRCES spares no effort in contributing to the Personal Integration of each member. Therefore, an aspect which is truly original with CIRCES is that its members are enabled to participate directly and individually in the common work of humanity, but always in perfect accord with their personal knowledge and aptitudes. In short, the personal experience of each member is brought to bear directly upon the Mission of CIRCES.

CIRCES consists of an Exoteric Outer Circle—the Circle of Doing—and an Inner Esoteric Circle—the Circle of Seeking. Therefore, the essential quality of a member of CIRCES is that of a true seeker and doer in his or her community. Each member of CIRCES is required to be actively engaged in some aspect of Cultural or Spiritual Research, be it a project to help the homeless, a project to reduce the need for violent action in the world, a program to improve the education of the world's children, or research into the Esoteric Sciences, or into the needs of our Senior Citizens. Membership in CIRCES is by no means passive!

CIRCES International, Inc.
Post Office Box 279
Plainfield, Indiana 46168

Forthcoming from CIRCES Books

Strange Encounters
by Raymond Bernard

That "there are more things in Heaven and Earth than are dreamt of in your philosophy, Dear Horatio" is, perhaps, one of the most profound and least appreciated truths of our time. However, the author of *Strange Encounters,* dares to relate a number of remarkable encounters which stretch the imagination and open to the reader possibilities beyond our current philosophies.

Secret Houses of the Rose-Croix
by Raymond Bernard

"Truth will touch the heart of him who is ready to receive it". So says Maha, one who has travelled the highways and byways of the sacred kingdom within. *Secret Houses of the Rose-Croix* is an account of those "inner places" which appeal to each aspirant according to his or her degree of understanding.

Secret Meetings in Rome
by Raymond Bernard

In this book Raymond Bernard describes a series of mysterious meetings in Rome which culminated in a meeting with "The Cardinal in White"—a man "whose unique stature in the Invisible Empire is such that he fills the role of pivot or hinge". Thus the door was opened to the author and the groundwork laid for the resurgence of the Order of the Temple (the OSTI) in the New Era.

Messages from the Celestial Sanctum
by Raymond Bernard
These "messages" treat a number of topics ranging from Visualization, through the Law of Silence, Psychic Powers and Reincarnation, to initiation and more. Above all the author presents a plan whereby each aspirant may attain to the highest spiritual levels but always in accord with his or her degree of understanding.

Ancient Wisdom in the New Era
by Onslow H. Wilson Ph.D.
Armed with the knowledge that each Era has its own unique signature, a specific "vibration" which impacts the inner consciousness of humanity, the author presents the essentials of Traditional Wisdom in modern garb. The result is a truly integrative approach to spiritual living in our modern world, in preparation for the Aquarian Age.

Feminine Initiation
by Jacques and Chantal Baryosher
Combining traditional and inspirational Qabalistic interpretations of the Feminine Principle, the authors use the stories of Ruth and Deborah of the Old Testament to convey the importance of The Feminine in each of us. Reflecting the current impact of The Feminine Principle in transforming human consciousness and reshaping human values, *Feminine Initiation* makes a strong case for The Feminine as the Hope for Humanity.

More Spiritual Classics from Globe Press Books

The Body of Light
History and Practical Techniques
for Awakening Your Subtle Body
by John Mann and Lar Short
A concise guide to the use of chakras for self-development. Reviews Hindu, Buddhist, Taoist and other traditions, and includes beginning, intermediate and advanced exercises, with over 60 illustrations. 1990. 192 pages, softcover, $12.95.

The Training of the Zen Buddhist Monk
by D.T. Suzuki
This is perhaps the best introduction to Zen and the life of the Zen monk. Forty-three illustrations by the monk Zenchu Sato depict many common practices in the life of the monks. 1991. 176 pages, 43 illustrations. Softcover, $9.95.

Dialogue on the Path of Initiation
An Introduction to the Life and Thought
of Karlfried Graf Dürckheim
by Alphonse Goettmann
"An eloquent tribute to one of the most profound spiritual teachers of our age. *Dialogue* can be an invaluable guide in the reader's search for transcendence and transformation."—Stanley Krippner, Ph.D. 1992. 192 pages, 17 photographs, softcover, $12.95.

On A Spaceship With Beelzebub
By A Grandson of Gurdjieff
by David Kherdian
A noted author tells the story of his own journey into and through the powerful Gurdjieff work of inner transformation. 1991. 288 pages. Hardcover, $24.95. Softcover, $12.95.

Self-Remembering
by Robert Earl Burton
A contemporary teacher of the Fourth Way shows the relation of self-remembering to every phase of the student's life and work. 1991. 232 pages. Hardcover, $40.00.

New Horizons
Explorations in Science
by P.D. Ouspensky
Explore the outer reaches of science with one of this century's greatest thinkers. Reprinted from *A New Model of the Universe,* these essays explain new outlooks on physics, the fourth dimension, mystical states of consciousness, and the study of dreams and hypnotism. With a new Introduction by Colin Wilson. 1990. 222 pages, softcover, $14.95.

Body Types
The Enneagram of Essence Types
by Joel Friedlander
Learn how to recognize the physical and psychological tendencies of each type. Explore the automatic thoughts, attitudes and motives of your type, and discover the dynamics behind your relationships. 1992. 192 pages, Softcover, $10.95.

Available at fine bookstores, or order direct from the publisher. To order or request a free catalog, send check, money order or complete Visa/MasterCard information and signature, along with $1.50 per item for shipping to:
Globe Press Books
P.O. Box 2045, Madison Station
New York, NY 10159.